Community College Studies

THE COMMUNITY JUNIOR COLLEGE

AN ANNOTATED BIBLIOGRAPHY

EMORY W. RARIG, JR., Editor

TEACHERS COLLEGE PRESS
Teachers College, Columbia University
New York

Library of Congress Catalog Card Number: 66–29990

Manufactured in the United States of America

Foreword

The Teachers College, Columbia University, Program for the Training of Administrators for Community and Junior Colleges was established March 4, 1960, with the aid of a grant from the W. K. Kellogg Foundation. The aims of the project are:

1. To prepare an increasing number of young administrators for the community and junior colleges.

2. To provide coordinated professional development (in-service and refresher) opportunities for persons already in administrative positions who may be interested either in improving their performance or in transferring to a new administrative position at a different level.

3. To provide a program of research and service.

In implementing these purposes, one of the first problems identified was the absence of an up-to-date, selective bibliography in the community junior college field. To help solve this problem, each member of two advanced seminars during the spring and autumn semesters of 1965 (taught by Professors Walter E. Sindlinger and Ralph R. Fields, respectively) demonstrated his exploration in one aspect of the community junior college by the presentation of an annotated bibliography. These were the primary source materials for this compilation.

The seminar students who submitted bibliographies were Robert Birnbaum, Richard J. Brower, Milton K. Erway, Frederick Q. Farr, Theodore N. Farris, Anna Fragnaud, Joseph N. Hankin,

John C. Harrington, William S. Hughes, Barbara LeBost, James J. Linksz, Joseph M. Mego, Edward D. Mills, Emory W. Rarig, Jr., Donald H. Smith, George C. Taylor, Don Wright, and Chih-Peng Yin.

The bibliographies were first brought together in a mimeographed document at the close of the spring semester, 1965, by Donald H. Smith and Emory W. Rarig, Jr., editors. The present printed work—enlarged with the autumn semester, 1965, bibliographies—was refined and edited by Mr. Rarig, Mr. Smith having returned to his full-time position as Dean of Curriculum and Instruction at Monroe Community College, Rochester, New York, at the end of the spring term.

It is hoped that this volume will be of some value to all those having need of such information. Since only those references are included that deal directly with the community junior college area, many of the major works in higher education have been excluded; on the other hand, many of the items included are listed more than once under different categories. The reader is cautioned to be aware that this effort represents merely a beginning. It is hoped that future seminars will continue to expand, refine, and update this work so that within a reasonable time it will become what was originally envisioned—a selective, annotated directory to the important community junior college literature and research works.

This is one in a planned series of publications to be produced by the Center for Community Colleges at Teachers College, Columbia University. It is hoped that this, and the others to follow, might make a small, yet significant, contribution to the most dynamic area in higher education today—the community junior college.

Walter E. Sindlinger
Director
Center for Community Colleges

March, 1966

Contents

The Community Junior College

Research Tools

(Sources of community and junior college facts and information for students and others interested in the movement.)

Alexander, Carter, and Arvid J. Burke. *How to Locate Educational Information and Data.* 4th ed., revised. New York: Teachers College Press, Teachers College, Columbia University, 1958. 419 pp.

Amid the flood of expanding knowledge, the need for this revised edition of the basic work is greater than ever. Presents concise procedures for utilizing the research facilities and the resources of the library, how to organize properly for research, and generally how to locate any educational materials in existence. An indispensable research tool in any field.

American Association of Junior Colleges. *Annual Report.* Washington, D.C.: The Association, published annually.

A yearly review of Association activities. Lists the officers, directors, staff, and commission members of the Association. Briefly summarizes Association activities in such areas as curriculum, publications, membership development, federal relations, and cooperation with universities.

American Association of Junior Colleges. *1965 Junior College Directory.* Washington, D.C.: The Association, 1965. 50 pp.

Published annually, this directory is a comprehensive, quick-reference guide to accredited two-year institutions in the United States. The current issue lists 719 institutions, an increase of 41 over the previous year. Criteria for listing in the directory consist primarily of regional or state accreditation. Statistical information includes enrollment figures for students and number of faculty members. For more detailed information the reader is directed to the 6th Edition of *American Junior Colleges,* published by the American Council on Education.

Boss, Richard D., and Roberta Anderson. *Bibliography on the Community-Junior College.* Corvallis, Ore.: The authors, 1965. Pagination not consecutive.

Unevaluated books and pamphlets are listed; a separate list of magazine articles published since 1955 is included. A supplementary list of articles often quoted and published prior to 1955 is valuable.

Community and Junior College *Catalogues* and *Bulletins.*

Issued yearly by individual colleges. Usually provides a history of the college, current calendar, curricula, degrees, costs, admission information, and other pertinent data.

Conley, William H., and Frank J. Bertalan. *Significant Literature of the Junior College, 1941–1948: An Annotated Bibliography.* Washington, D.C.: American Association of Junior Colleges, 1949. 40 pp.

Contains annotated references to significant articles, books, and doctoral theses from the period indicated. A categorized author index according to twenty-one areas is very helpful.

Education Directory, 1964–1965: Part 3, Higher Education. Department of Health, Education, and Welfare, U.S. Office of Education. Washington, D.C.: Government Printing Office, 1965. 237 pp.

Lists all institutions of higher education in the United States that offer at least a two-year program of college-level studies in residence and are accredited or approved by a nationally recognized accrediting agency, or by a state department of education. Hence most of the community and junior colleges are listed, with their location, administrative officers, main curricula, and various summarizing tables.

Elam, Stanley, ed., and others. *Research Studies in Education, 1963.* Bloomington, Ind.: Phi Delta Kappa, 1963. 163 pp.

This monograph, published by the professional fraternity for men in education, provides information concerning doctoral dissertations under way and doctoral dissertations completed, an author index, and a research methods bibliography. Works are listed by author and classified according to subjects, among which "Junior College; Community College" is included as one of the categories.

Eskow, Seymour. *Barron's Guide to the Two-Year Colleges.* Great Neck, N.Y.: Barron's Educational Series, 1960. 370 pp.

Provides valuable information for prospective college students and their parents. Part I sets forth guidelines for the prospective student for self-appraisal regarding motives, interests, chances of success, financial ability, and academic proclivity; Part II gives helpful hints for approaching the various programs available; and Part III provides a directory of the two-year colleges in the United States with capsule information about each one, including a map locating each college.

A Fact Book on Higher Education. American Council on Education, Office of Research, comp. Washington, D.C.: The Council (updated four times each year). 269 pp. + index.

A looseleaf handbook published by the Council and kept current by quarterly issues of replacement pages. Covers just about all the statistical facts about higher education one would need to have at his fingertips. Includes such areas as enrollments, foreign students, adult enrollments, labor force, research expenditures, gross national product, endowment figures, salaries in higher education, graduates, degrees granted, and many others. Also serves as a source of selected and unusual educational information, such as statistics on loans to students in higher education under the National Defense Education Act, selected continuation ratios and estimated retention rates, and direct federal support of students in higher education. A very rich reference source for higher educational information.

Gage, N. L., ed. *Handbook of Research on Teaching.* Chicago: Rand McNally & Company, 1963. 1218 pp.

While not dealing directly with two-year colleges, this volume does provide valuable summaries of research work being conducted in many areas of vital interest to these colleges. This is especially true of Chapter 23, "Research on Teaching at the College and University Level," by W. J. McKeachie (pp. 1118–1172), which deals with such topics as motivation, feedback, variability and verbalization, and research on teaching methods.

Gleazer, Edmund J., Jr., ed. *American Junior Colleges.* 6th ed. Washington, D.C.: American Council on Education, 1963. 551 pp.

Standard directory of two-year colleges; contains exhibits and descriptive materials on 655 junior colleges recognized by regional or state accrediting agencies. Included are such items as enrollments, curricula, admission and graduation requirements, control, accreditation, history, calendar, fees, staff, library, publications, finances, and administration. This volume, together with the publication *American Universities and Colleges,* provides a rather complete directory of all higher educational institutions in the United States.

Harris, Chester W., ed. *Encyclopedia of Educational Research.* 3rd ed. New York: The Macmillan Company, 1960. 1564 pp.

Presents a quick, but clear and thorough, review of current research being conducted in various phases of education. The article in this edition on "Junior Colleges," by James W. Reynolds, gives a sharp focus to the types of research being done at the time (1958) with brief summaries and interpretive trends.

Junior College Journal. Published eight times each year by the American Association of Junior Colleges (Roger Yarrington, Editor). Washington, D.C.: The Association.

The official organ of the American Association of Junior Colleges. Contains current happenings, reports of studies, scholarly articles, information about new books, placement, and so forth in the junior college world. With its new, modernized format since 1963, it ranks among the finest in professional journals.

Meeth, L. Richard, ed. *Selected Issues in Higher Education: An Annotated Bibliography.* New York: Teachers College Press, Teachers College, Columbia University, 1965. 212 pp.

A ready reference manual in which laymen and professional educators can quickly find desired sources of information on a wide range of prominent educational issues. While dealing with higher education in general, many of the issues for which annotated references are provided are pertinent to those interested in two-year college issues as well. An educational tool of unusual and timely value.

Morrison, D. G., Ken August Brunner, and S. V. Martorana. *The 2-Year Community College: An Annotated List of Unpublished Studies and Surveys, 1957–1961.* Bulletin 1963, No. 28, Department of Health, Education, and Welfare, U.S. Office of Education. Washington, D.C.: Government Printing Office, 1963. 41 pp.

This small booklet lists sources and materials not usually available in other research references and follows a similar publication made in 1958. The two items together provide a comprehensive reference source for many of the studies under way or completed in the two-year college area for a ten-year period. The 270 studies listed in the 1963 work are classified for convenience into such categories as administration, finance, testing, and curriculum.

Padfield, William T. *A Bibliography of Selected Publications Related to Junior College Education.* Sacramento, Calif.: California State Department of Education, 1965. 75 pp. Mimeographed.

Provides an up-to-date source of annotated journal references in five specified areas of study: (1) evaluation of college instruction, (2) grading practices and assignment of marks in college,

(3) motivation in the junior college and college classroom, (4) learning theories and their practices, and (5) counseling in junior colleges and colleges.

Parker, Franklin, Anne Bailey, and William K. Ogilvie, compilers. *The Junior and Community College: A Bibliography of Doctoral Dissertations, 1918–1963.* Washington, D.C.: American Association of Junior Colleges, 1965. 47 pp.

Listing over 600 dissertations completed in the community junior college field, this publication fills a long-recognized need. The dissertations are indexed under subject headings: Administration, Instructional Programs, Student Personnel Services, and so forth. This classification helps to emphasize the relative amount of research that has been done in each of the classifications.

I. A History of the Community Junior College

A. THE BEGINNINGS

Angell, James R. "The Junior College Movement in High Schools." *School Review,* 23:289–302, May, 1915.

Presenting an early history of the movement, this author claims that the impetus for present development came not from the "occasional university leaders" but from the secondary schools and "from the intelligent public that supports them." He is convinced that communities may demand that junior colleges be sensitive to local needs (and not just copy the first two years of the conventional college curriculum).

Blauch, L. E. "Reorganization on European Lines Appears Imminent." *School Life,* 9:77–79, December, 1923.

Junior colleges are compared with early liberal arts studies in the Renaissance that laid a broad general foundation for later work with faculties of law, medicine, and theology. The article presents a good discussion of the early academy as a transitional school.

Brown, J. Stanley. "Present Development of Secondary Schools According to the Proposed Plan." *School Review,* 13:15–18, January, 1905.

Discussion of credits and "advanced standing" of students accepted at colleges for work done in the fifth and sixth years of Joliet High School, Joliet, Illinois.

Brush, H. R. "The Junior Colleges and the Universities." *School and Society,* 4:357–365, September 2, 1916.

This author noted the trend of the junior college toward having an individuality of its own—being not merely an appendix to the high school nor a prefix to the upper classes of the university. He states that "the junior college will attract the vocational student once it has developed an individuality of its own."

Folwell, William Watts. *University Addresses.* Minneapolis, Minn.: H. W. Wilson Company, 1909. 224 pp.

Contains Folwell's 1869 inauguration address as president of the University of Minnesota, in which he recommends transferring "the body of work for the first two years in our ordinary American colleges" to the secondary schools. Personal comments (p. 38) indicate that this idea came from a professor of his at Columbia College (Charles A. Joy) who had studied in Germany and had explained the German educational system to Folwell in the early 1850's.

Harper, William Rainey. "The High School of the Future." *School Review,* 11:1–3, January, 1903.

This article reiterates the proposal for the general reorganization of education in the form of a six-year elementary and a six-year secondary school. The author discusses the arguments for and against such a system.

Harper, William Rainey. "President's Annual Report." *Decennial Publications of the University of Chicago—1900–1902.* Chicago: University of Chicago, 1903. Pp. 1–143.

President Harper discusses extensively his views on the junior college. The sections entitled "Affiliation and Cooperation," "The Junior College," and "Philosophy of Separation" are most important for an understanding of the movement.

Harper, William Rainey. *President's Annual Report, July, 1898–July, 1899.* Chicago: University of Chicago, 1900. Pp. 20–21.

Trustees of the University of Chicago voted to confer "the title or degree of Associate" on those students who finish the work of the junior college. Consideration and results of this action are discussed by Harper.

Harper, William Rainey. "The Small College—Its Prospects." *Journal of Proceedings and Addresses of the 39th Annual Meeting of the National Education Association, Charleston, South Carolina, 1900.* Chicago: University of Chicago Press, 1900. Pp. 67–87.

Strong arguments for and against the small colleges are presented. Changes expected and desired are: strengthening of some, reducing others to academies, and modifying others into junior colleges (pp. 81–87). This address was also printed under the title *The Prospects of the Small College,* by the University of Chicago in 1900, 46 pp.

Hedgepeth, V. W. B. "The Six-Year High School Plan at Goshen." *School Review,* 13:19–23, January, 1905.

Early example of six-year high school offering junior college work because of student demand, not just as an experiment. Correspondence and agreement by the Goshen Board of Education with William Rainey Harper is included.

Hinsdale, Burke A. *History of the University of Michigan.* Ann Arbor, Mich.: The University of Michigan, 1906. 376 pp.

In his inaugural address as president of the University of Michigan, Henry Tappan suggested (pp. 43–44) the advisability of the transfer of the work of secondary depth of the university to the high school (1852), thus preparing for the junior college plan.

Jordan, David Starr. "The College and the University." *Science,* 27:530–533, April 3, 1908.

This article is an extract from Jordan's 1906–07 President's Report at Stanford University in which he discusses the purposes of the original endowment for Stanford. He concludes that the entrance requirements must be met after completion of comparable junior college work since the "university must be relieved from the burden of elementary instruction."

Koos, Leonard V. *Integrating High School and College: The Six-Four-Four Plan at Work.* New York: Harper & Brothers, 1946. 341 pp.

The historical development as well as the details of the six-four-four plan are considered in this work.

Lange, Alexis Frederick. "The Junior College as an Integral Part of the Public School System." *School Review,* 25:465–479, September, 1917.

An address given before secondary school representatives at the University of Chicago on April 10, 1917. Three questions are asked: "Shall certain colleges have their heads cut off—?" "Shall the American university have its legs cut off—?" "Shall the American four-year high school be stretched, and if so, how?" The last question is answered "yes," the stretching to be done by the junior colleges.

Lange, Alexis Frederick. "A Junior College Department of Civic Education." *School and Society,* 2:442–448, September 25, 1915.

The author proceeds to lay down functions for junior colleges: (1) a middle vocational school; (2) organic part of a high school having preparatory curriculum; (3) intimate relationship to social progress of the community during the entire period of adolescence of pupils.

Lange, Alexis Frederick. "The Junior College with Special Reference to California." *Educational Administration and Supervision,* 2:3–8, January, 1916.

Details of the influence in the early movement of David Starr Jordan, who urged the "amputation of freshman and sophomore classes to prevent university atrophy." Jordan gave general currency to the name "junior college," which proved much more potent in suggestible communities.

McDowell, Floyd Marion. *The Junior College.* Department of the Interior, U.S. Bureau of Education, Bulletin No. 35, 1919. Washington, D.C.: Government Printing Office, 1919. 139 pp.

Chapter 2 (pp. 10–15) documents the "Origin and Early Development of the Junior College"; while Chapter 3 (pp. 16–39) explores "Influences Tending to Further the Development of the Junior College Idea."

Report of the Committee of the National Council of Education on Economy of Time in Education. Department of the Interior, U.S. Bureau of Education, Bulletin No. 38, 1913. Washington, D.C.: Government Printing Office, 1913. 106 pp.

This report concludes that the general college course could end at age 20 (instead of 22) if there were greater efficiency of subject matter in the earlier grades in elementary and secondary schools.

Sachs, Julius. "The Elimination of the First Two College Years—A Protest." *Educational Review,* 30:488–499, May, 1905.

"On what evidence would we receive into our upper classes more satisfactory students than have hitherto reached the freshman year?" The normal attainments of secondary school teachers teaching in a six-year high school will produce an unreliable product.

Tappan, Henry P. *The Progress of Educational Development.* Ann Arbor, Mich.: The University of Michigan, 1855. 51 pp.

This article traces the philosophical and historical basis of our colleges and universities. Dr. Tappan counsels the leading institutions to strike out boldly to form true universities—"and each establish by its own side a proper gymnasium."

Tappan, Henry P. *University Education.* New York: G. P. Putnam's Sons, 1851. 120 pp.

A philosophical and historical review of the origins of university education. Herein is presented an eloquent plea for the establishment of a "true" university surrounded by two-, three-, or four-year colleges.

B. ERA OF DEVELOPMENT

Bogue, Jesse P. *The Community College.* New York: McGraw-Hill Book Company, 1950. 390 pp.

A comprehensive treatment of the history, purposes, organization, and problems of the community junior college.

Bogue, Jesse P., and Shirley Sanders. "Analysis of Junior College Growth." *Junior College Journal,* 19:311–319, February, 1949.

A documented analysis of the growth of junior colleges to 1948. The authors believe that Lewis Institute, founded in Chicago in 1896, was the first private two-year college; the first public junior college was Joliet Junior College, organized in 1902.

Boren, Claude B. "Why a Junior College Movement?" *Junior College Journal,* 24:345–357, February, 1954.

Considers such social factors contributing to the movement as (1) changing composition of population, (2) technology, (3) popularization of secondary school education, and (4) increasing complexity of society.

Brick, Michael. *Forum and Focus for the Junior College Movement: The American Association of Junior Colleges.* New York: Teachers College Press, Teachers College, Columbia University, 1964. 222 pp.

"The literature of higher education pays scant attention to the history of the junior college movement." Chapters 1 and 3 present the development of the junior college movement in the socio-economic and educational context. Throughout the book, attention is paid to the pioneers of the movement and their ideas.

Campbell, Doak S. "After Sixteen Years." *Junior College Journal,* 7:221–229, December, 1936.

In 1920 only the North Central Association of Colleges and Secondary Schools published and provided means for administering standards for junior colleges. By 1936, all regional associations worked with these institutions. This is a historical study of the maturing of two-year colleges.

Colvert, C. C. "Half-Century of Junior Colleges." *Junior College Journal,* 17:244–247, February, 1947.

The Lewis Institute of Chicago is identified as the first junior college (1896).

Cooper, William John. "The Junior College Movement in California." *School Review,* 36:409–422, June, 1928.

California's superintendent of public instruction outlines the history of the movement from its birth (prior to 1907), to infancy (1907), to adolescence (1917–1921), to youth (1921–1928). States that geography of state rather than educational leadership was responsible for first legislation (1907) making possible post-high school work in the public schools.

Coulter, Ellis Merton. *College Life in the Old South.* New York: The Macmillan Company, 1928. 381 pp.

The trustees of Franklin College (now the University of Georgia) formally adopted a plan to eliminate the first two years of college work in 1859; freshman and sophomore work would be given in the Collegiate Institute (a *gymnasium*).

Cowley, William H. "The War on the College." *Atlantic Monthly,* 169:719–726, June, 1942.

The University of Chicago on January 22, 1942, announced that it would grant the bachelor's degree at the end of the sophomore year. The junior colleges in 1942 tended to oppose the granting of bachelor's degrees to students who completed two years of college; their position, backed by the presidents of numerous four-year colleges, helped to prevent the wider application of Hutchins' proposals.

Cox, R. G. "Retrospect and Prospect." *Junior College Journal,* 1:27–36, March, 1931.

The author emphasizes the diversity of junior colleges and the hope that each junior college's policy will show an interest in adapting to the needs of the community or the constituency which it serves.

Davis, J. B. "Looking Backward and Forward After 25 Years." *Junior College Journal,* 9:126–131, May, 1939.

This article is a historical analysis of the 25 years prior to 1939 with special emphasis on the curriculum of public and private two-year colleges.

Eells, Walter C. "Abolition of the Lower Division: Early History." *Junior College Journal,* 6:193–195, January, 1936.

An extremely interesting and well-documented article which gives the University of Georgia credit for being the first American institution to reach the decision to eliminate freshman and sophomore work from the university.

Eells, Walter C., ed. *American Junior Colleges.* 1st ed. Washington, D.C.: American Council on Education, 1940. 585 pp.

This was the initial authoritative listing of accredited junior colleges. The institutional data are preceded by a brief history of junior colleges. Succeeding editions of this standard directory have been published in 1948, 1952, 1956, 1960, and 1963.

Eells, Walter C. *The Junior College.* Boston: Houghton Mifflin Company, 1931. 833 pp.

This book presents a monumental comprehensive view of the entire junior college field. Chapters 3, 4, and 5 (pp. 44–159) give an excellent description of the junior colleges' historical development, in California and elsewhere.

Eells, Walter C. *Present Status of Junior College Terminal Education.* Washington, D.C.: American Association of Junior Colleges, 1941. 340 pp.

Second in a series of fine monographs by the Commission on Junior College Terminal Education. A historical review of the terminal function is developed in Chapter 2.

Fretwell, Elbert K., Jr. *Founding Public Junior Colleges: Local Initiative in Six Communities.* New York: Teachers College Press, Teachers College, Columbia University, 1954. 148 pp.

Describes the establishment of six public junior colleges in their respective community settings. Emphasizes the importance of local initiative, by both individuals and organized groups, in pushing forward to bring greater higher educational opportunities to their young people. Concludes with some common factors and suggested general procedures for establishing public junior colleges.

Houston, G. David. "The Junior College of the Future." *Education,* 48:401–409, March, 1928.

Historical summary of the movement dating back to 1839. Four ways of developing junior colleges are defined: (1) cut the university in half, (2) reduce four-year colleges to two years, (3) establish normal schools, and (4) add two years to high school.

Ingalls, Roscoe C. "The Inaugural Address—'Purposeful Pioneers.'" *Junior College Journal,* 5:238–245, February, 1935.

Ingalls, the director of the Los Angeles Junior College, writes in praise of William Henry Snyder—creator of the local college. Snyder is proclaimed a pioneer in the development of a new type of education by bringing together the liberal arts college and vocational school.

Johnson, B. Lamar. "Junior College Trends." *School Review,* 52:606–610, December, 1944.

An excellent study of the growth of junior colleges over a twenty-year period. A clear analysis with five key trends in the movement given.

Johnson, Paul L. *Community College Education: A Book of Readings.* Doctor of Education Project Report, Teachers College, Columbia University, 1951. 2 vols. 669 pp. Typewritten.

An analysis of the community college prior to 1951 is well documented in the chapter (pp. 1–16) on "Getting a Perspective on the Community College."

Kirchgessner, Florence. "The Junior College." *Catholic Educational Review,* 22:153–162, March, 1924.

A general survey of junior college developments in the United States, tracing the Catholic junior colleges back to 1677 because the early preparatory seminary course included two years of instruction beyond the high school.

Koos, Leonard V. *The Junior College Movement.* Boston: Ginn & Company, 1925. 436 pp.

The history of the development of the junior college movement until 1925 is discussed in Chapter 1 (pp. 1–15) of this older, well-written work. This material appeared earlier as Bulletin No. 5 from the University of Minnesota (1924).

Koos, Leonard V. "Rise of the People's College." *School Review,* 55:138–149, March, 1947.

The author indicates that the first reference to the junior college as "the people's college" was in 1875 in Minneapolis by William Watts Folwell, first president of the University of Minnesota. Folwell advocated developing in that state a system of secondary schools that would include the first two years of college.

Learned, William S. "Junior College, the University, and the Community." *Carnegie Foundation for the Advancement of Teaching, 29th Annual Report.* New York: The Foundation, 1934. Pp. 21–35.

The junior college is described as an institutional development necessary to the logic of our American educational system. This staff member of the Carnegie Corporation also discusses the junior college as an instrument of general education.

Long, Winifred R. "Analysis of Junior-College Growth." *Junior College Journal,* 16:226–232, February, 1947.

In a study of junior college growth covering a 25-year period, it is noted that the total enrollment of about 16,000 students found in 1922 had increased to over 400,000 in 1947. A good statistical study.

Noffsinger, H. G. "One-Third of a Century of Progress." *Junior College Journal,* 5:395–404, May, 1935.

A few of the salient features of the movement included in this article are Harper at Chicago, Tappan at Michigan, Folwell at Minnesota, and James at Illinois (an earlier try in Pennsylvania failed). The title of the article refers to Harper's annual report in 1902.

Reynolds, James W., ed. *Junior College Journal,* 25:425–485, April, 1955.

The entire issue is devoted to discussion of the past twenty-five years of the junior college movement. Significant developments are treated in separate articles.

Roland, L. J. "The American Junior College." *Social Education,* 22:357–360, November, 1958.

This author discusses the history of the junior college, both private and public, in the United States. He indicates that junior colleges were established, among other reasons, to meet expressed community needs not supplied by other agencies.

Ross, H. "University Influence in the Genesis and Growth of Junior Colleges in California." *History of Education Quarterly,* 3:143–152, September, 1963.

Brief scholarly summary of the influence of the German university on the junior college movement in America in the late nineteenth and early twentieth centuries. Detailed study of the movement in California up to the present time.

Rudy, Willis. *The Evolving Liberal Arts Curriculum: A Historical Review of Basic Themes.* New York: Teachers College Press, Teachers College, Columbia University, 1960. 135 pp.

Beginning with the Yale Report of 1828, the author traces the evolution of the liberal arts curriculum through the era of developing specializations. The historical trends at various colleges throughout the country are examined as they relate to the balance between the elective and prescriptive courses. Perhaps the future path lies toward the infusion of the liberalizing spirit into all teaching.

Sack, Saul. "The First Junior College." *Junior College Journal*, 30:13–15, September, 1959.

Claims that Susquehanna University (Pennsylvania), as the Missionary Institute of the Evangelical Lutheran Church, began life as a junior college (1858) with the conscious purpose of remaining so. It became a four-year college in 1895.

Seashore, Carl E. *The Junior College Movement*. New York: Henry Holt & Company, 1940. 160 pp.

A study of the "rootlets" of the junior college is presented in this article. The author's thesis is that European secondary schools influenced the early development of junior colleges.

Sexson, John A., and John W. Harbeson. *The New American College*. New York: Harper & Brothers, 1946. 312 pp.

A history of the six-four-four plan. The book is of particular interest because it draws similarities and contrasts between the four-year and the two-year college movements.

Smith, L. W. "Founding of Early Junior Colleges—President Harper's Influence." *Junior College Journal*, 11:511–521, May, 1941.

An excellent piece of historical research on Harper's influence in the junior college movement.

Ward, Phebe. *Terminal Education in the Junior College*. New York: Harper & Brothers, 1947. 282 pp.

A very useful history of the early development of "terminal" curricula in the two-year colleges, particularly in California.

Whitney, Frederick L. *The Junior College in America*. Colorado Teachers College Education Series No. 5. Greeley, Colo.: Colorado State Teachers College, 1928. 258 pp.

A valuable sourcebook of statistics that proves helpful after the 1925 study by Koos and before the 1931 study by Eells.

Wood, J. M. "Twenty Years' Progress." *Junior College Journal*, 10:257–263, May, 1940.

The president of Stephens College discusses the growth of private and public two-year colleges from 1920 to 1940. He wants these schools to permit as many young men and women as possible to continue their education.

Zook, George F. *National Conference of Junior Colleges, 1920, and First Annual Meeting of the AAJC, 1921.* Department of the Interior, U.S. Bureau of Education, Bulletin No. 19, 1922. Washington, D.C.: Government Printing Office, 1922. 73 pp.

From the period when the junior college received a "forum and focus" through the birth of the American Association of Junior Colleges.

C. THE CONTEMPORARY SCENE

Blocker, Clyde E., Robert H. Plummer, and Richard C. Richardson, Jr. *The Two-Year College: A Social Synthesis.* Englewood Cliffs, N.J.: Prentice-Hall, 1965. 298 pp.

A well-written, up-to-date sociological analysis of the junior college, the technical institute, and the university branch in their respective environments.

Clark, Burton R. *The Open Door College: A Case Study.* New York: McGraw-Hill Book Company, 1960. 316 pp.

An approach to the character of a junior college, to "show how this character was determined, and to indicate its consequences." It represents a sociological analysis of the first four years of San Jose Junior College in California. A central consideration in the study is the manner in which the wishes of the students affect the character of the college.

Diekhoff, John S. *Democracy's College.* New York: Harper & Brothers, 1950. 208 pp.

Presents the relationship between the community and the colleges designed to serve the community.

Fields, Ralph R. *The Community College Movement.* New York: McGraw-Hill Book Company, 1962. 360 pp.

A clear, detailed analysis of the past, present, and future of the community college through theoretical and practical considerations. The book starts with the development of the two-year college, continues through its transition to a full-scale community college, and culminates with four examples of currently active community colleges with outstanding, but also quite different, programs. Special attention is focused on the critical problems facing the community college today.

Fretwell, Elbert K., Jr. "New York: The Next Five Years." *Junior College Journal,* 33:22–25, March, 1963.

A discussion of some of the major considerations in the expansion of community colleges in New York State. The author, presently dean of academic development of the City University of New York, identifies problem areas for immediate attention.

Gleazer, Edmund J., Jr., ed. *American Junior Colleges.* 6th ed. Washington, D.C.: American Council on Education, 1963. 551 pp.

A systematic, scholarly reference work which includes an introduction to the junior colleges and specific information on over 650 accredited two-year institutions.

Hamilton, Thomas, and Edward Blackman, eds. *The Basic College of Michigan State.* East Lansing, Mich.: The Michigan State College Press, 1955. 127 pp.

Although it is a part of a major university, the Basic College of Michigan State University and the development of its program provide insights for two-year college general education programs.

Hillway, Tyrus. *The American Two-Year College.* New York: Harper & Brothers, 1958. 276 pp.

This volume is a valuable combination of the treatment of the place of the junior college in our contemporary society and a down-to-earth guide for the organization, financing, and operation of this educational unit. A documented account of the history of community colleges is given in the second chapter (pp. 33–60), "The Development of the Two-Year College."

Johnson, B. Lamar. *General Education in Action: A Report of the California Study of General Education in the Junior College.* Washington, D.C.: American Council on Education, 1952. 409 pp.

This is the classic study of general education in the junior colleges of California. Descriptions and very brief histories of each of the California public two-year colleges are given.

Keppel, Francis. "Standards of Excellence." *Junior College Journal,* 34:8–11, September, 1963.

A presentation of several points for viewing the two-year college's past achievements and future role. The former U.S. Commissioner of Education asserts that we must strive for quality of education and breadth of opportunity in higher education.

McConnell, T. R. *A General Pattern for American Public Higher Education.* New York: McGraw-Hill Book Company, 1962. 198 pp.

A broad-gauge development of the past, present, and future of American public higher education. The author coordinates the present trends and issues, defines the major problems, and then presents a general pattern for the future. While he stresses the major position of the university, diversity as a major element is equally important. The two-year college, as a part of that diversity, is dealt with in Chapter 7 (pp. 110–135), "The People's College."

McGrath, Earl J. *The Future of the Community College.* Mid-Winter Lecture Series, School of Education, The University of Buffalo. Buffalo, N.Y.: Partners' Press, 1962. 13 pp.

A clear, concise delineation of the current problems and challenges that face the community colleges, with some valuable implications for the future.

Medsker, Leland L. *The Junior College: Progress and Prospect.* New York: McGraw-Hill Book Company, 1960. 367 pp.

In this study of seventy-five two-year institutions in fifteen states, Medsker addresses himself to the basic question: Is the community college really a unique institution serving special functions which other institutions cannot serve effectively? In the process, the author turns a searching eye at the development of the two-year colleges in the various states and appraises their strengths and weaknesses.

The Public Junior College. Fifty-fifth Yearbook of the National Society for the Study of Education, Part I. Chicago: The Society, 1956. 347 pp.

The entire yearbook is devoted to a comprehensive study of the rationale for the two-year college. Among the authorities contributing are B. Lamar Johnson, Paul Dressel, Ralph R. Fields, Jesse Bogue, James Reynolds, and Lawrence Bethel.

Smith, Leo F., and Laurence Lipsett. *The Technical Institute.* New York: McGraw-Hill Book Company, 1956. 319 pp.

Although technical institutes have existed in the United States for over 100 years, here is the first attempt to bring together much of the information about technical institute education. Also provided are projected techniques for organizing, administering, and evaluating technical programs.

Thornton, James W., Jr. *The Community Junior College.* New York: John Wiley & Sons, 1960. 300 pp.

Traces the origins and the historical development of the junior college concept; examines its philosophical bases; and shows how this college represents a response to changes in American society.

Wattenbarger, James L., and Winfred L. Godwin, eds. *The Community College in the South: Progress and Prospects.* A Report of the Committee on Education Beyond the High School, Southern States Work Conference. Tallahassee, Fla.: State Education Department, 1962. 132 pp.

The objective of the committee was to examine the diverse needs of an expanding student potential at the post-high school level in order to suggest patterns of operation and methods of study which each of the southern states might consider in attempting to solve their problems. Among the problems attacked were state-wide planning, goals, legal status of junior colleges, and trends in development of community junior colleges.

II. Functions and Purposes of the Community Junior College

Beckes, Isaac K. "The Case for Community Junior Colleges." *Junior College Journal,* 34:24–30, April, 1964.

In building his case for community colleges as the best means of meeting post-high school educational needs at the community level, the author deals with the functions or roles of the college, including (1) the function of providing low-cost education, (2) the necessity for comprehensiveness in offerings, (3) emphasis on the teaching function.

Besse, R. M. "Education and the Race Problem." *Junior College Journal,* 35:3–7, October, 1964.

Deals with the ways in which public junior colleges can aid in the drive for equality on the part of Negro groups. Such aid is discussed in terms of (a) vocational and technical education beyond the high school, (b) the admissions standards of public junior colleges, (c) the curriculums offered in such colleges, and (d) adult educational opportunity.

Bogue, Jesse P. *The Community College.* New York: McGraw-Hill Book Company, 1950. 390 pp.

An excellent basic text that provides a great deal of understanding of the community college movement, including functions and purposes of the two-year institution.

Bogue, Jesse P. "The Needs of Junior Colleges in an Expanding Role." *Junior College Journal,* 28:305–306, February, 1958.

The author raises three questions that bear vitally on the role of the junior college: (1) How well are the students being educated? (2) How wisely are they being counselled and guided? (3) How realistically are curriculums being organized to meet the demands of the coming years?

Campion, Howard A. "The Junior College Must Hold Open the Closing Door of Opportunity for Higher Education." *Junior College Journal,* 31:511–512, May, 1961.

Clearly pointed out in this article is the fact that with the increasing demand for higher education and the resulting selectivity of four-year colleges and universities, the junior college has become the only open door to higher education for an increasing number of individuals.

Campion, Howard A. "The Role of the Junior College in Higher Education." *College and University,* 35:426–434, Summer, 1960.

Discusses the place of the junior college in the California Master Plan of 1960. Deals with the purposes of the community colleges and some of the problems in the way of achieving these purposes in California.

Clark, Burton R. *The Open Door College: A Case Study.* New York: McGraw-Hill Book Company, 1960. 316 pp.

This work selects for intensive observation a recently established junior college—San Jose Junior College in California. The author discusses the problems inherent in the achievement of an organizational identity and role. Of special value is his treatment of the ways in which the junior college handles the "latent terminal" student.

Colvert, C. C. "The Expanding Role of the Junior College." *Junior College Journal,* 28:245–246, January, 1958.

This essay deals with the role of the junior college in program planning, students, plant, and guidance. The necessity for the reorganization of college districts to serve larger areas and broaden the financial base to fulfill the above roles is discussed.

Crawford, W. H., and H. M. Roitan. "The Junior College Challenge of the Sixties." *Junior College Journal,* 31:183–188, December, 1960.

This article warns that the pressure of the sixties will result in an emphasis on selective admissions in junior colleges and a swing to the more traditional collegiate type of program. The only way to guard against these developments is close scrutiny of basic philosophy and wise planning both at the local and at the state level.

Daughtrey, J. P. "Vision of the Junior College Future." *Junior College Journal,* 29:465–468, April, 1959.

The vision of the junior college of the future here given is that of a "preparatory college" serving the distinctive function of preparing its students for a mature adulthood within a Christian, democratic frame of reference and recognized as an independent unit in an interrelated educational system. This system would have the flexibility necessary to develop its own curricular program without penalizing those students who will transfer to upper-division educational institutions.

Derthick, L. G. "The Expanding Role of the Junior College." *Junior College Journal,* 28:185, December, 1957.

A concise statement on the role of the junior college in broadening educational opportunity, providing strong guidance and counselling programs, developing pre-professional programs in basic fields, adapting to occupational changes and providing for vocational training, providing a necessary common core of general education for all students, and supplying adult education.

Erbstein, George B. "Informal Non-Credit Adult Education in the Public Community Junior College: Current Trends and Future Prospects." Doctor of Education Project Report, Teachers College, Columbia University, 1962. 257 pp. Typewritten.

A very informative study dealing with what many consider to be a central role of the community college—community service. The author concludes on the basis of his investigations that, while the non-credit function of such programs is continuing and will expand, it occupies a position of subsidiary importance to the other phase of adult education—degree credit courses.

Fields, Ralph R. *The Community College Movement.* New York: McGraw-Hill Book Company, 1962. 360 pp.

Captures the mood of the community college movement through a descriptive technique. The description consists of the history of the movement from its beginnings, its essential characteristics, and a detailed description of four community colleges. In the last section, basic issues are pointed up—issues that bear on the success of the community college in meeting its goals.

Fretwell, Elbert K., Jr. "New York: The Next Five Years." *Junior College Journal,* 33:22–25, March, 1963.

This knowledgeable article (1) looks at the size of the job to be done in New York State by two-year colleges, (2) points out some of the chief problems that hamper the college in meeting its goals, (3) proposes that attention be given to certain additional areas for the more effective functioning of the junior college.

Gleazer, Edmund J., Jr. "Our Emerging Profile." *Junior College Journal,* 34:3–4, May, 1964.

The suggestion by Willard Wirtz that compulsory education should be extended for two more years is discussed, and the key role of the community junior college in extending educational opportunity is pointed out. The author suggests thirteen points that should be considered in the emerging profile of the public junior college.

Goldberg, Arthur J. "Education for Freedom and Equality." *Junior College Journal,* 36:6–10, September, 1965.

The present United States Ambassador to the United Nations suggests that education for freedom has as one of its aspects "individual self-fulfillment," as well as active participation in democratic governance. He suggests that, regardless of mental ability, the family income level seems largely to dictate whether a young person does or does not go to college. Here is only one way in which the junior colleges exercise a democratizing influence. Further democratizing effects are presented by the author, who is one of the Chicago Junior College's most distinguished alumni.

Harris, Norman C. *Technical Education in the Junior College: New Programs for New Jobs.* Washington, D.C.: American Association of Junior Colleges, 1964. 102 pp.

This clearly written and excellently illustrated work presents the different technical opportunities that are open to properly prepared personnel. It focuses on the great need for trained people to fill these jobs and highlights the role of the junior college in providing that training.

Johnson, B. Lamar. *General Education in Action: A Report of the California Study of General Education in the Junior College.* Washington, D.C.: American Council on Education, 1952. 409 pp.

One of the functions of the public junior college is to provide general education. This work discusses the importance of this function, the goals of general education, and the operation of a program of general education.

Johnson, Paul L. "Community College Education: A Book of Readings." Doctor of Education Project Report, Teachers College, Columbia University, 1951. 2 vols. 669 pp. Typewritten.

Deals with problems and issues in community college education and analyzes them by surveying the literature. Chapter 1, "Understanding the Composite Nature and Purposes of the Community College," is especially pertinent.

Lindsay, F. B. "Junior Colleges in Higher Education." *Junior College Journal,* 28:125–131, November, 1957.

Sets forth the dictum that the primary function of the junior college is not training for advanced study at a college or a university, nor for employment in an occupation. It is general education for citizenship to enable its graduates to participate intelligently in community, state, national, and world affairs.

Littlefield, Henry W. "America's Stake in the Junior College." *Junior College Journal,* 31:483–491, May, 1961.

Deals with the role to be played by the junior college in an era of struggle for survival and pinpoints those items considered essential as functions of the junior college: (1) democratization, (2) equalization of educational opportunity, (3) efficient utilization of manpower, (4) the transfer function, and (5) the development of desirable personality traits.

Littlefield, Henry W. "Critical Issues Facing America's Junior Colleges." *Junior College Journal,* 31:361–364, March, 1961.

While the author concerns himself primarily with the identification of critical issues that face junior colleges, he also lists the different roles of the junior college that, when taken together, make it a unique institution.

McCall, R. C. "How Does the Comprehensive Community Junior College Promote Scholastic Excellence?" *Junior College Journal,* 31:533–536, May, 1961.

An insistent plea for the achievement of excellence in scholarship as a function of the junior college. This achievement must not be allowed to deteriorate because of involvement with numbers or because of concern for salvaging marginal talent.

McConnell, T. R. *A General Pattern for American Public Higher Education.* New York: McGraw-Hill Book Company, 1962. 198 pp.

Of special interest to those examining the community college movement is Chapter 7 (pp. 110–135), "The People's College." The place of the California junior colleges in the state plan is described; the success of the colleges in meeting the goals of transfer students is examined; and the problem of what to do for the exceptional student is discussed.

Meany, George. "Labor and the Community College." *Junior College Journal,* 34:6–8, February, 1964.

This appeal for expansion of the publicly supported community college by the president of the AFL-CIO indicates some of its "raisons d'être": (1) to make certain that higher education will be possible for the less wealthy and less brilliant student; (2) to help transmit our rapidly growing cultural, intellectual, and scientific heritage to future generations; (3) to provide occupational training; (4) to provide pre-university education; (5) to provide for citizenship; and (6) to provide remedial work.

Medsker, Leland L. "Diversity, a Fact and a Responsibility." *Junior College Journal,* 28:505–513, May, 1958.

An excellent panoramic view of the role of the two-year colleges and their impact on higher education as a whole. Because of the two-year colleges, (1) opportunity for higher education is broadened; (2) provision is made for expanded curricular offerings; (3) special community services are afforded; (4) guidance is stressed; (5) articulation with both the high school and the senior college is essential; and (6) adequate academic standards are a necessity.

Medsker, Leland L. *The Junior College: Progress and Prospect.* New York: McGraw-Hill Book Company, 1960. 367 pp.

Describes the functions of the two-year college as they actually are discharged, and compares the functions performed with the claims commonly made by this type of institution.

Muirhead, Peter P. "The Junior College Must Assist in an Important Way to Discharge Society's Obligation to Put Higher Education Within Financial Reach of All Qualified Students." *Junior College Journal,* 31:513–518, May, 1961.

It is pointed out that the vitality of the two-year college flows from the unique service it performs—that of providing a wide variety of educational programs, seldom available elsewhere, to a wide diversity of students at a cost within their means. The author shows the relationship of federal programs of financial assistance to the two-year college in achieving this goal.

National Advisory Committee on the Junior College. "Junior Colleges—A Policy Statement." *Education Digest,* 30:39–42, March, 1965.

A statement emphasizing the role of the junior college in providing middle-level job education to meet the needs for specialized manpower and to help solve some of the most critical problems in American society today—poverty and unemployment, social and ethnic unrest.

Neilan, E. P. "The Changing Educational Scene: Community Colleges May Hold the Key to Future Economic Growth." *Junior College Journal,* 34:4–8, October, 1963.

The basic point made by the author is that since the community college offers an opportunity for training a substantial portion of the necessary manpower, it holds the key to economic growth.

Nunis, Doyce B., Jr., and R. M. Bossone. "Junior College's Search for an Educational Identity." *Junior College Journal,* 33:121–124, November, 1962.

A re-examination and re-evaluation of the purposes and functions of the junior college are pursued in an attempt to assist the junior college in finding its true educational identity in the field of higher education. Ten recommendations are made to assist in this task.

Parker, Franklin. "Community Junior College, Enfant Terrible of American Higher Education: A Bibliography of 225 Doctoral Research Dissertations." *Junior College Journal,* 32:193–204, December, 1961.

In a foreword to this listing of 225 doctoral research dissertations on the community junior college, the author discerns three developing stages in the history of the junior college movement: the acceptance of the junior college as an appropriate institution for offering the first two years of approved baccalaureate programs, acceptance of terminal and semiprofessional functions, and acceptance of service to the community as a function of the junior college. Also discussed is the view that the junior college, peculiarly American, is the offspring of democracy.

The Public Junior College. Fifty-fifth Yearbook of the National Society for the Study of Education, Part I. Chicago: The Society, 1956. 347 pp.

A volume that would be unfairly described in just a few sentences; it is a gold mine of thought-provoking concepts within and without the community college movement. Chapter 4 in Section I, on "The Role of the Public Junior College," is especially relevant.

Reed, Dell, and H. S. Bonar. "What Future Role for the Junior and Community College?" *Bulletin* of the National Association of Secondary-School Principals, 43:69–74, April, 1959.

This report of a discussion on the future role of the junior and community college suggests a drastic expansion of such colleges to meet the needs of American youth for their first two years of higher education. Such expansion would permit the four-year colleges and universities to specialize in senior college and graduate level work.

Richards, Maxwell J. "An Analysis of the Technical Education Provided by the Accredited Junior Colleges." *Junior College Journal,* 28:105–108, October, 1957.

A report of the results of a survey dealing with the technical curriculums offered by public junior colleges accredited by regional or state agencies. The author concludes that accredited junior colleges have oriented themselves quite well to the demands of technical education.

Sarko, Laura. "The Problem of Teaching in Community Colleges." *Journal of Higher Education,* 35:384–386, October, 1964.

The author maintains that the two-year community college course was designed to "provide a transitional discipline to full intellectual maturity and academic adequacy." The conditions which hinder the success of the college in playing its role are the low overall quality of the student body and the lack of autonomy in the community college. The key to success is the development of real traditional academic freedom for faculty and administrative officials.

Sheats, Paul H. "The Junior College and the Educative Community." *Adult Education,* 9:94–97, Winter, 1959.

Suggests that the community college deal with the problem of adult education not with a traditional approach, but with one that utilizes the community and community resources for the solution of problems that concern the local citizenry.

Shriver, Robert Sargent. "The Role of Junior Colleges in the Intellectual War." *Junior College Journal*, 28:365–367, March, 1958.

Suggests that the two-year colleges forget the word "junior" and concentrate on the better word "community." Given adequate resources of teachers, tools, space, and time, the community colleges can help America to win the "intellectual war."

Thornton, James W. *The Community Junior College*. New York: John Wiley & Sons, 1960. 300 pp.

This fine work deals first with the philosophy and place of the junior colleges; second, with the organization and administration of junior colleges; third, with the junior college curriculum; and fourth, with student personnel problems in the junior college. Chapter 5, "The Future of the Community Junior College," is especially relevant to considerations of function and purpose.

Tickton, Sidney G. "What's Ahead for Public Junior Colleges." *Junior College Journal*, 34:9–11, November, 1963.

Tickton projects present enrollment figures into the future and concludes that the junior colleges will have to function quite differently from the way they do today in order to fulfill their roles. Better utilization of time, space, and personnel are essential; and especially essential to all three of these is long-range planning.

"The 2-Year College for Women: A Challenge Met." *New York Times*, March 7, 1965, Sec. 12, pp. 1–16 (entire section).

Sponsored by twenty-four two-year colleges for women, this supplement highlights a phenomenon of our time—that nearly 50 per cent of the girls graduating from high school go on to college. The two-year college for women is particularly adapted to serve its students. Prefaced with a message from the U.S. Commissioner of Education, the unique challenges to faculty and students are set forth. The twenty-four colleges participating in the report are members of the Conference of Two-Year Colleges for Women, which is affiliated with the American Association of Junior Colleges.

Vaccaro, Louis C. "The Manpower Development and Training Act and the Community College." *Junior College Journal,* 34:21–23, November, 1963.

The commonly accepted functions of public community junior colleges are set forth and the ways in which such functions relate to the Manpower Development and Training Act are pointed out. The functions indicated are transfer function, terminal course offerings, remedial course offerings, community services function, and guidance services function.

Valade, W. J. "The Community College Ideal." *Junior College Journal,* 28:332–336, February, 1958.

The author isolates the concept of the community college and establishes some criteria by which the ideal community college can be more readily identified. On the basis of a review of the literature, the author thinks that a college is progressing to the goal of an ideal community college to the degree that it fulfills six criteria which have to do with the fulfilling of community needs.

Walsh, J. P. "Manpower Development: A Junior College Responsibility." *Junior College Journal,* 34:8–12, May, 1964.

The deputy director of the Office of Manpower, Automation, and Training in the U.S. Department of Labor points up the major problems and challenges in the nation's manpower situation. Despite great prosperity, unemployment persists; for the solution to this problem, education, training, and job creation are necessary. It is suggested that future growth in employment will be in areas that can best be served by occupationally oriented programs in a sophisticated scheme of vocational-technical education that the junior college offers.

Ward, Phebe. *Terminal Education in the Junior College.* New York: Harper & Brothers, 1947. 282 pp.

In 1940 the American Association of Junior Colleges and the General Education Board of New York City initiated a one-year study to explore the field of terminal education, followed immediately by a four-year continuation study. The accumulated data from these two studies constitute the bases for this report.

From the data, institutional reports, and publications emanating from these studies, principles of terminal education are evolved; these in turn are followed by suggested procedures for developing terminal education programs in junior colleges. Among the areas for which suggested procedures are given are: community surveys, use of community resources, curricula, cooperative work programs, guidance, and testing. This work is a classic in the field of junior college literature.

Wardlaw, H. P., and J. G. Fox. "What is Today's Role for the Junior or Community College?" *Bulletin* of the National Association of Secondary-School Principals, 42:85–88, April, 1958.

In this treatment of the variety of functions performed by the junior college, the suggestion is made that: "One way American society may be better served would be for high schools, junior colleges and universities to turn out more efficient students and by better counseling methods see that those who cannot succeed in college are channeled into productive pursuits."

Wheeler, Helen Rippier. "The Community College Library: An Appraisal of Current Practice." Doctor of Education Project Report, Teachers College, Columbia University, 1964. 220 pp. Typewritten.

A survey of 198 public community colleges in 27 states with the stated purpose, ". . . to identify and describe the ways in which the community college library can and should best serve its unique institution's program."

White, Ruth W. "The Role of the Community College Library." *Junior College Journal,* 33:109–111, October, 1962.

The proper role of the community college library raises many questions of policy. Often library policy develops with little or no plan. This author maintains that the key to the effective community college library lies in cooperation—with the faculty, with the administration, with students, with the public, and with other libraries in the area. Real cooperation means working together toward a common goal; this article suggests some aspects of this spirit in the operation of the community college library.

Williams, Glenn D. "Junior College: New Opportunities in Higher Education." *Clearing House*, 36:102–104, October, 1961.

A general statement dealing with the usefulness of the junior college to American society and to individual Americans.

III. Organization and Administration of Community Junior Colleges

A. ORGANIZING

Brumbaugh, A. J. *Guidelines for the Establishment of Community Junior Colleges.* Atlanta: Southern Regional Education Board, n.d. 21 pp.

Reviews the community junior college movement: origin, development, and philosophy. The importance of formulating criteria for the establishment of community colleges is emphasized. Eight criteria are presented and discussed; general guidelines are developed concerning the nature and role of the community junior college and basic information which should be collected and evaluated in any state or community in which such establishment is being considered.

Establishing Junior Colleges. Occasional Report Number 5, UCLA Junior College Leadership Program. Los Angeles: University of California, Los Angeles, 1964. 145 pp.

The founding of a new college is an exceedingly complex operation; there has been very little, however, written to provide useful information on how to start a junior college. As the number of community and junior colleges opening each year increases, the need for specific directions and guidelines becomes critical. The knowledge of "how to do it" lies chiefly in the experiences of those able administrators who themselves have founded a college. Hence, it was the purpose of the conference reported by this publication to bring together those authorities in the community junior college field who had experience in the organizing of a new college. The report covers such important areas as steps and time sequences, organizing student personnel services in new junior colleges, providing plant facilities, securing and organizing the staff, developing community relations, and developing the curriculum. The addition of actual case reports makes this a most valuable, practical document.

Johnson, B. Lamar. *Starting a Community Junior College*. Washington, D.C.: American Association of Junior Colleges, 1964. 91 pp.

An eminent authority in junior college education calls attention to the many far-reaching decisions that must be made in the early stages of planning a new community junior college. Often these decisions must be made under extreme pressure, and under trying conditions of inadequate personnel and facilities. In an effort to assist in establishing some order in the process, Johnson has set up a taxonomy of steps to be taken in each of the areas of operation that are important in starting a community junior college: curriculum, student personnel services, staff, finance, plant and facilities, and community services.

Morrison, D. G., and S. V. Martorana. *Criteria for the Establishment of 2-Year Colleges*. Bulletin 1961, No. 2, Department of Health, Education, and Welfare, U.S. Office of Education. Washington, D.C.: Government Printing Office, 1961. 101 pp.

The results of a survey of professional opinion and of state studies relative to desirable criteria are reported. From an analysis of these, guidelines are proposed to be followed in developing criteria for the establishment of 2-year colleges. A state-by-state summary of legal and regulatory provisions is included in the appendix. This is an indispensable blueprint for all those involved in the establishment of community junior colleges.

President's Commission on Higher Education. *Higher Education for American Democracy, Volume III: Organizing Higher Education*. Washington, D.C.: Government Printing Office, 1947. 74 pp.

Chapter 2, "Developing Adequate Facilities" (pp. 5–23), suggests functions and guidelines for organizing community colleges. In order to achieve its purposes, the community college must be organized to provide at least for: (1) community surveys to identify needs, (2) cooperative work programs, (3) a well-integrated (general and vocational) program, (4) programs for transfer, and (5) adult education programs. The commission clearly delineates the "special role" of the junior college and recommends that state surveys be conducted, that permissive legislation be enacted, and that state-wide master plans be developed. It is also recommended that the possibilities of closer articulation between the high schools and the colleges, both two-year and four-year, be explored; and that the organization of community colleges should be designed to benefit the state as well as to serve their respective communities.

B. FINANCING

Badger, Henry Glenn. *Junior College Accounting Manual.* Washington, D.C.: American Association of Junior Colleges and American Council on Education, 1945. 128 pp.

While manuals of accounting procedures had been developed for the public schools and for colleges and universities, until the time of this publication none had been specifically prepared for the junior college. Hence junior college accounting could be described as a borrowed or adapted system. The present manual, while old, is a standard reference work dealing with the problems that arise and methods of dealing with them as well as presenting the specialized forms and accounts needed.

Blocker, Clyde E., Floyd S. Elkins, and Fred H. Bremer. *Philanthropy for American Junior Colleges.* Washington, D.C.: American Association of Junior Colleges, 1965. 34 pp.

In past years, philanthropy in support of junior colleges has not been significant. The authors, for purposes of this study, identified six criteria important in fund-raising and compared the philanthropic records of those junior colleges possessing these criteria to a marked degree with those not exhibiting these criteria. Among the conclusions reached was the fact that the employment of a development officer by a college was perhaps the most important influence toward improving its philanthropic income.

A Comprehensive Summary of Federal Loans, Grants, and Contracts in Health, Education, and Welfare Programs as of the Fall of 1964. New York: Tamblyn & Brown, 1964. 28 pp.

Drawn together in a single booklet is a summary of information about federal loans, grants, and contracts available to institutions (including community and junior colleges) in the fields of health, education, and welfare. Although all of the information appears in various other sources, the publishers have performed a distinct service in aggregating it into one source, which is of value to anyone concerned with programs in his college that might qualify for federal aid.

Eldridge, Donald A. "Developing Financial Resources." *Junior College Journal,* 35:28–31, October, 1964.

A college president describes the blueprint he has followed in achieving fund-raising success. The author sets forth some of the basic principles and techniques he has learned, among them having a sound philosophy of education, seeking faculty help and enthusiasm, soliciting parental enthusiasm, careful timing, employing professional consultants, and utilizing volunteers. He concludes with five "simple" suggestions for fund-raising success.

Hungate, Thad L. *Finance in Educational Management of Colleges and Universities.* New York: Teachers College Press, Teachers College, Columbia University, 1954. 202 pp.

This volume is a standard work on the philosophy, procedure, and practice of the financial management of educational institutions, including community junior colleges. The development of a "philosophy of support" represents a concept of creative leadership; the procedures are clear, concise, and practical.

Hungate, Thad L. *Management in Higher Education.* New York: Teachers College Press, Teachers College, Columbia University, 1964. 384 pp.

One of the truly significant works of our time in administrative theory and practice. Covers all phases of the management of higher education, including functions, policies, and philosophies. Emphasis is placed on the functions of management, with special implications for long-range planning. Of special value is a section relating to state organization and responsibility for higher education.

While this work does not deal specifically with the junior or community college, it does bring a lifetime of valuable experiences in higher education to bear on all of the problems of higher educational management, including those of the community junior colleges, the four-year institutions, and the universities.

Morrison, D. G., and S. V. Martorana. *State Formulas for the Support of Public 2-Year Colleges.* Bulletin 1962, No. 14, Department of Health, Education, and Welfare, U.S. Office of Education. Washington, D.C.: Government Printing Office, 1962. 70 pp.

The statutory provisions for state, local, and student shares in supporting current operating expenses and capital outlay are presented. Statutory and regulatory provisions for the support of two-year institutions are given state by state.

Timmins, Richard H. "Fund Raising in Junior Colleges." *Junior College Journal,* 33:3–6, September, 1962.

Although junior colleges have been in the fund-raising business for a long time (1903), the author points out that all too often the work done by junior colleges in fund-raising has been overshadowed by the efforts of large, four-year institutions. Identified sources of funds for junior colleges are corporations and business concerns, religious denominations, governing boards, individuals and friends, alumni, general welfare foundations, nonalumni and non-church groups, and other sources. Timmins wisely points out that the four-year institutions do not have a monopoly on the gift market; that "money will be forthcoming when the public is convinced of the institution's value."

C. LEGISLATION

Commission on Legislation of the American Association of Junior Colleges. *Establishing Legal Bases for Community Colleges.* Washington, D.C.: The Association, 1962. 43 pp.

Growing out of a conference sponsored by the Commission on Legislation of the American Association of Junior Colleges, this report focuses attention on approaches to establishing legal bases in two major areas: financing public community colleges, and patterns of control of community colleges. The appendices, which present recent state legislation information and an exhibit of a general enabling act, are especially valuable.

Commission on Legislation of the American Association of Junior Colleges. *Principles of Legislative Action for Community Junior Colleges.* Washington, D.C.: The Association, 1962. 18 pp.

Presents seven basic principles of legislation for community junior colleges as developed by the Commission. Valuable to members of state legislatures, state boards, citizens' committees, and laymen interested in establishing increased opportunities for higher education.

Hollis, Ernest V., S. V. Martorana, and Jeanne D. Brandt. *Survey of State Legislation Relating to Higher Education: January 1, 1963, to December 31, 1963.* Department of Health, Education, and Welfare, U.S. Office of Education. Washington, D.C.: Government Printing Office, 1964. 274 pp.

This annual publication presents (Part I) a summary of the state legislation relating to higher education passed during the year and (Part II) a digest of the legislation considered state by state. Usually included in each of the yearly issues are some observations on apparent trends in legislation enacted, together with some implications from legislation that was unsuccessful in passage.

Kirschbaum, Sheila. *Federal Legislation Affecting Junior Colleges.* Washington, D.C.: Commission on Legislation, American Association of Junior Colleges, n.d. 13 pp.

A small but most valuable booklet that summarizes the new educational legislation passed by the 88th Congress of the United States as it relates to junior colleges. Reviewed are such acts as the Economic Opportunity Act of 1964 (P.L. 88-452), NDEA Amendments of 1963 (P.L. 88-210), Nurse Training Act of 1964

(P.L. 88-581), the Higher Education Facilities Act of 1963 (P.L. 88-204), and the Vocational Education Act of 1963 (P.L. 88-210).

D. THE URBAN COMMUNITY COLLEGE

Coultas, Walter T. "Problems of the Urban Junior College." *Junior College Journal*, 35:13–16, October, 1964.

The assistant superintendent of the Los Angeles City School District describes some of the problems involved in maintaining seven community colleges serving 69,000 students in a typical urban complex of today. Dealing with concentrated minority groups, special programs for low achievers, creation of a favorable image, and the difficulty of coordination among the autonomous units of the complex are some of the major problems in the urban community college complex.

Jensen, Arthur M. "Urban Community Colleges Go Multicampus." *Junior College Journal*, 36:8–13, November, 1965.

A study that examines the role of the central office and the individual campuses of the multicampus district. It looks at the reasons for, the types of organization used in, and some of the administrative policies and practices related to multicampus operations.

The author states that to the spring of 1964, ten multicampus systems had been established. Since that time three more have been established and at least six others are projected. He predicts that the "majority of the multicampus districts will eventually become multicollege districts."

Mayhew, Lewis B., and others. *Community Colleges in Urban Settings.* Community College Planning Center, Western Regional Center, School Planning Laboratory. Stanford, Calif.: School of Education, Stanford University, 1964. 20 pp.

A report of the suggestions growing out of a two-day conference on urban community colleges. It describes the significance of urban life and how the community college might share in that significance and then offers some guides for planners contemplating an urban setting for their community colleges to implement this goal.

Rarig, Emory W., Jr., comp. *Report of the Urban Community College Planning Conference.* Center for Community Junior College Administration. New York: Teachers College, Columbia University, 1964. 49 pp. Mimeographed.

A report of a two-day conference held at the Greyston Conference Center of Teachers College concerning the problems of urban community college administration. Using an interdisciplinary approach, authorities presented their views on approaches to the establishment and administration of community colleges and their branches in the large urban complex. Attended by the major community college administrators in the United States associated with large urban settings, the conference culminated in the identification of a number of problem areas and suggested modes of action to approach them.

E. GENERAL

Blocker, Clyde E., and Henry A. Campbell. *Attitudes of Administrators Toward the Administrative Organization of Public Junior Colleges in Seven States.* Austin, Texas: The authors, 1962. 41 pp.

The purpose of this study was to determine, through an examination of the concepts and attitudes of two-year college administrators, the most appropriate organization for administering such colleges. The general conclusion was that community college organizational structure will be most appropriate when it conforms to the needs of the people of the community. Since this is a variable of unusual dimension, no organizational structure can be identified as "best" in any general way.

Fordyce, Joseph W. "Creating a Good Climate." *Junior College Journal,* 35:17–20, December, 1964–January, 1965.

The Chairman of the AAJC Commission on Student Personnel suggests in this article that an institution's most important public is its student body. The favorable influence exerted by students in behalf of the college toward parents, taxpayers, and prospective students is very great. The author suggests that a serious look at our junior college personnel policies is in order in light of this consideration. He contends that a sincere and honest concern for the welfare of the students is the foundation upon which a good institutional climate is created.

Garrison, Roger. "Effective Administration for Superior Teaching." *Junior College Journal,* 32:517–525, May, 1962.

The college owes each teacher "a genuine on-going vital educational experience on the level of challenge to his professional abilities." The author also believes that it is a prime administrative responsibility to have a college that is a learning place for teachers. He discusses in an interesting manner the things college administrators can do to create a congenial, stimulating context for faculty learning.

Harris, Norman C. "Administrative Leadership in Vocational-Technical Education." *Junior College Journal,* 32:380–387, March, 1962.

The community college president looks at his expected leadership role on the campus, in the community, and in his profession. This article deals with a rationale for vocational-technical problems in two-year colleges.

Kintzer, Frederick C. *Presidents' Reports in American Junior Colleges.* Occasional Report No. 4, UCLA Junior College Leadership Program. Los Angeles: University of California, Los Angeles, 1963. 70 pp.

While the form of the reports of junior college presidents varies widely, there are certain broad similarities. Approximately one-half of their content deals with the student activities and the business affairs of the college. Among the findings of this study of 292 presidents' reports from community and junior colleges are many valuable suggestions for administrators, board members, and laymen. For example, the use of this type of document to popularize the college and gain public support is relatively new; the study gives some interesting insights into the values to be derived from using it in this way.

McGrath, Earl J. *The Future of the Community College.* Buffalo, N.Y.: Partners' Press, 1962. 13 pp.

Given as the Mid-Winter Lecture at the University of Buffalo, in March, 1961, this booklet presents a very clear statement of the role of the community college in American higher education, together with some of its problems and its opportunities.

Martorana, S. V., and Ernest V. Hollis. *State Boards Responsible for Higher Education.* Department of Health, Education, and Welfare, U.S. Office of Education. Washington, D.C.: Government Printing Office, 1960. 254 pp.

In addition to survey information on 209 state boards responsible for public higher education in the United States, this U.S. Office of Education document gives a thorough state-by-state description of the organizational structure of public higher education. Basic reference tables also give the types of institution for which these state boards are responsible. This is a very valuable handbook on state organization for higher education for researchers and laymen as well as administrators.

Nance, Paul K., Leslie F. Robbins, and J. Harvey Cain. *Guide to College and University Business Management.* Bulletin 1965, No. 30, Department of Health, Education, and Welfare, U.S. Office of Education. Washington, D.C.: Government Printing Office, 1965. 169 pp.

In addition to requirements for technical competence in fiscal management, the professional college business manager has a unique role in that his primary concern is in the efficient utilization of funds in keeping with the objectives of the college. With this perspective, the authors discuss the nine major functions of the professional college business manager as well as several other shared functions. A checklist for evaluating college and university business management is an especially valuable section at the end of the document.

Pray, Francis C. "A PR Trilogy." *Junior College Journal,* 34:16–20, November, 1963.

There is no such thing as "The" junior college; rather there are individual institutions. This is how they are thought of by the supporting public. Working from this view, the author develops three basic points to remember in gaining increased understanding and support for the junior colleges. The starting point is to involve in the activities all those groups related to public relations: the trustees, the faculty, the students, and the alumni. He suggests that a fund-raising program is a good vehicle for "friend raising."

Sindlinger, Walter E. "Variety Among Junior and Community Colleges." *From High School to College: Readings for Counselors.* New York: College Entrance Examination Board, 1965. Pp. 27–34.

The so-called American higher education system has always been characterized by its great diversity of institutions. The community junior college is diversified in many ways: differences in names, in administrative structure, in programs offered, and in many other areas. Sindlinger points out that it is this very diversity that gives the community junior colleges their vitality in reflecting the needs of varying communities in which they are located and from which they derive their support.

IV. Community Junior College Students

Clark, Burton R. *The Open Door College: A Case Study.* New York: McGraw-Hill Book Company, 1960. 316 pp.

Contains interesting data on ability levels of students entering California community junior colleges, on attrition rates, and on faculty attitudes toward their college and students. Specific organizational, curriculum, personnel, and student counselling problems caused or accentuated by an open-door admissions policy are discussed.

Community College Research Symposium: The Community College Student. Proceedings of a symposium held in Seattle, Washington, February 8–9, 1963. Olympia, Wash.: State Superintendent of Public Instruction, 1963. 34 pp.

Two research papers on the community college student in the state of Washington and a discussion of each are given. Among the many problems discussed, both papers identified the need for exploring ways of "getting to" those students who, amid a helpful faculty, competent counsellors, and a complete library, nevertheless will not seek help or advice. The motivation-guidance-career decision process emerges as the real problem area.

Facing Facts about College Admissions. Newark, N.J.: The Prudential Insurance Company of America, 1962. 27 pp.

One of a series of unusually clear, concise, and factual booklets on higher education distributed by the Prudential Insurance

Company. This one serves as an excellent guide for pre-college students and their parents.

Facing Facts about College Costs. Newark, N.J.: The Prudential Insurance Company of America, 1962. 28 pp.

Another very fine booklet in the Prudential series. This one presents college cost projections to aid parents and students in facing the problem of financing a college education with realism and foresight.

Facing Facts about the Two-Year College. Newark, N.J.: The Prudential Insurance Company of America, 1963. 31 pp.

Another in the Prudential series, this booklet shows pre-college students and their parents how the two-year college can help them in solving their higher educational problems. Very attractive charts, maps, and tables help to portray the role of the community junior college clearly and accurately.

Kastner, Harold H., Jr. "Student Deficiencies and the Community College Dilemma." *Junior College Journal,* 30:140–142, November, 1959.

Remedial courses are necessary to correct deficiencies of students entering an open-door community college, since each student in the regular transfer or technical program must receive the preparation necessary to transfer to a four-year college or to enter a specific technical occupation. Stringent academic requirements are considered to be perhaps even more important for technical students than for the transfer students because those who complete only two years may be forced to compete with college graduates for jobs in all but the most technical and specialized areas.

Knoell, Dorothy M., and Leland L. Medsker. *From Junior to Senior College: A National Study of the Transfer Student.* Washington, D.C.: American Council on Education, 1965. 102 pp.

Report of a study of 7,243 junior college students who transferred to four-year institutions in 1960. In student characteristics, this transfer group was found remarkably similar to the native student population in the four-year colleges. A majority of these students had taken a general or college preparatory course and had ranked in the upper half of their high school class. Economic factors seemed to be the major consideration in their decision to attend a junior college as freshmen, such as low tuition and the opportunity to live at home with parents, thus reducing housing and food costs.

McDaniel, J. W. *Essential Student Personnel Practices for Junior Colleges.* Washington, D.C.: Student Personnel Commission, American Association of Junior Colleges, 1962. 54 pp.

An excellent guide for those responsible for the student personnel programs in community colleges. Describes desirable practices; indicates the methods to be used, the jobs to be done, and the responsibilities involved. Also provides guidelines for organizing the junior college student personnel program.

Metcalf, Alan W. *Community College Student Characteristics.* Olympia, Wash.: State Superintendent of Public Instruction, 1965. 34 pp.

This report represents the first part of a two-year study concerned with the attrition problem. Consisting of a compilation of student characteristics in the state of Washington, it projects a hypothetical community college that embodies those characteristics. This model then represents the typical student body of the state.

Mohs, Milton C. *Service Through Placement in the Junior College: The Organization and Operation of a Junior College Placement Bureau.* Washington, D.C.: Student Personnel Commission, American Association of Junior Colleges, 1962. 102 pp.

Another excellent guide from the Student Personnel Commission of the AAJC, which highlights the need, organization, and operation of placement services in the junior colleges. Of special value are the appendices, in which there appear actual exhibits of the various forms that have been used successfully by junior colleges.

O'Connell, Alfred C. "The Open-Door College: A License to Fail?" *Junior College Journal,* 21:241–242, January, 1961.

The tenet expressed here is that only students who are determined and have a reasonable probability of success should be admitted to transfer programs. Students not meeting this requirement should be counselled out of considering a transfer program, or required to take remedial work before being permitted to enter the regular program. Several reasons for this proposal are discussed, such as the psychological harm of failure and the public relations aspects of high attrition rates.

Plummer, Robert H., and Richard C. Richardson, Jr. "Broadening the Spectrum of Higher Education—Who Teaches the High-Risk Student?" *Journal of Higher Education,* 35:308–312, June, 1964.

It is suggested that to avoid the problems of faculty hostility, too wide a range of student abilities in community college classes, and a profusion of courses which mars the image of the community college, the curriculum must be reorganized to provide an academic division for transfer and technical programs (with selective admissions, faculty rank, and all instruction on the college level), and a service division (unrestricted admission, no college credit given, variable length of courses to fit students and subject matter). Movement between the two curriculums must be kept open.

Schenz, Robert F. "What is Done for Low Ability Students?" *Junior College Journal,* 34:22–27, May, 1964.

Results of a survey to determine what community colleges are doing for low-ability students. Findings indicate that 91 per cent of the sample of 185 colleges attempted to identify low-ability students; that the commonest definition of low ability was a score below the 15th percentile on tests with national norms; that 10 per cent of the public colleges will not admit low-ability students; that half of the public institutions admitting low-ability students place them on probation at admission; that 89 per cent of these schools provide some sort of special instruction for these students; and that two-thirds of the colleges had never performed a study to determine the relative success of low-ability students in their programs.

Schultz, Raymond E. "The Impact of Academic Probation and Suspension Practices on Junior College Students." *Junior College Journal,* 32:271–275, January, 1962.

Data gathered from twenty-seven colleges selected on the basis of the relatively restricted or liberal nature of their academic regulations indicated that variations in these policies did not appear to affect student motivation. Data indicate that of students placed on probation after one semester of work, 35 per cent failed to return to the institution within five years; 51 per cent of those who did return were not successful the second semester. Fewer than 10 per cent of those placed on probation graduated within five years. These data indicate the "revolving door" nature of open-door policies.

Smith, George B. *Who Would Be Eliminated?* Kansas Studies in Education, Vol. 7, No. 1. Lawrence, Kan.: University of Kansas, 1956.

An analysis of what the 1955 graduating class at the University of Kansas (which has an open-door admission policy) would have looked like had a relatively modest admissions criteria (a score above the 50th percentile on the A.C.E.) been used to select students. Of 1,006 graduates, 245 (24.4 per cent) would not have met this requirement.

Smith argues that the open-door policy thereby saved a large number of students who would not have otherwise been able to attend college.

Wells, Herman B., John A. Perkins, and G. Russell Clark. *The Legislature and Higher Education in New York State.* New York: Academy for Educational Development, December, 1964. 65 pp.

Report by the New York State Legislature Consultant on Higher Education indicating the need for expanded facilities in the state. Chapter 8 notes that students in the top three-fourths of their high school graduating classes are generally able to find educational opportunities in the state, but suggests a growing need for providing higher education for students in the lowest quarter. The establishment of "Youth Colleges" to serve this purpose is proposed.

V. Community Junior College Programs

A. GENERAL EDUCATION

Bogue, Jesse P. *The Community College.* New York: McGraw-Hill Book Company, 1950. 390 pp.

The author laments the dichotomy between general education and vocational education and attempts to show the relationship between the two. In Chapter 7 (pp. 151–178), he sets forth basic principles for the development of general education in community colleges, including sample curriculums offered by three community colleges (Bradford, Chicago City, and Pine Manor junior colleges). Chapter 8 (pp. 179–205) contains much data on the integration of general education with technical (vocational) education offered in community colleges.

Dressel, Paul L., ed. *Evaluation in General Education.* Dubuque, Iowa: William C. Brown Company, 1954. 333 pp.

A series of reports on the practices in evaluating the general education curriculum at thirteen junior colleges and four senior colleges and universities. Of great value to all administrators concerned with the evaluation of general education because of the detailed procedures included—for example, the evaluative procedures used at Chicago City Junior College and Antioch College. Explains how this evaluation can be translated into better instruction.

Eckert, Ruth E. *Outcomes of General Education: An Appraisal of the General College Program.* Minneapolis, Minn.: University of Minnesota Press, 1943. 210 pp.

A report of a project which evaluated the effectiveness of the two-year program in general education offered to students of limited scholastic ability by the General College of the University of Minnesota. Traces the specific objectives of the general education curriculum; the attitudes, interests and abilities of the students; the anticipated changes in the students; and the actual changes evident in the students.

General Education in Community Junior Colleges. Proceedings of the Annual Florida Junior College Conference held at Florida State University, Tallahassee, October 1–2, 1959. Tallahassee, Fla.: State Department of Education, 1959. 99 pp.

Consists of five addresses by well-known experts on various aspects of general education, and the proceedings of four discussion sessions which transpired at the Annual Junior College Conference at Tallahassee in 1959. Virtually all of this report will prove of value to the educational administrator, especially those sections concerned with the relationship of junior college programs in general education to the biological sciences, the humanities, the physical sciences, and the social sciences. Gives insights into the organization and practices of general education in the Florida junior colleges.

Hofstadter, Richard, and C. DeWitt Hardy. *The Development and Scope of Higher Education in the United States.* New York: Columbia University Press, 1952. 254 pp.

Chapter 8 compares general education and liberal education, noting the ambiguity encountered in defining these terms; explores the philosophical concepts behind liberal and general education; and traces the origin of general education as it arose out of the attempts to reconcile the natural sciences with liberal education. Chapter 3 (pp. 57–100) deals, in part, with the role of general education in graduate and professional education. While not dealing directly with the two-year general education program, the book does have many important overall implications for this area.

Johnson, B. Lamar. *General Education in Action: A Report of the California Study of General Education in the Junior College.* Washington, D.C.: American Council on Education, 1952. 409 pp.

A classic study of policies and practices in the general education curriculum of the junior colleges of California. The book is divided into four parts: goals of general education, general education programs in action, administration of the programs, and persistent problems and opportunities facing the general education programs. It emphasizes the functional approach in planning and developing the general education curriculum, and the importance of counselling and guidance in assembling data that can directly shape the general education program.

Johnson, Roy Ivan, ed. *Explorations in General Education.* New York: Harper & Brothers, 1947.

An analysis of the general education program offered at Stephens College and of the processes and methods whereby this curriculum evolved and is evaluated. The program is predicated on the belief that "learning becomes a search for understanding rather than the amassing of unrelated facts." Especially noteworthy are the chapters on a basic course in the humanities, education for marriage, and the program in communication skills. The faculty's practices in solving problems which arose in this program are analyzed.

Mayhew, Lewis B., ed. *General Education: An Account and Appraisal.* New York: Harper & Brothers, 1960.

A masterly work of great value to the administrator, this volume is precisely what it purports to be—a practical guide for college faculties to the administration, organization, and evaluation of the general education program. Included are chapters whose objective is the improvement of the institution's existing program of general education; curriculum problems, methodology, and teaching materials; and the development of a faculty dedicated to the general education program. The book concludes with an analysis of the current problems, current changes and innovations, and the future trends of the general education curriculum.

Medsker, Leland L. *The Junior College: Progress and Prospect.* New York: McGraw-Hill Book Company, 1960. 367 pp.

A succinct summary of the general education practices and philosophy in seventy-six representative junior colleges located in fifteen states may be found in Chapter 3 (pp. 55–63). In addition to enumerating the objectives of these general education programs, the author treats them in a rather iconoclastic fashion, noting that 77 per cent of the colleges "relied primarily on conventional or departmental courses to meet their responsibilities for general education"—only 30 per cent "had established courses specifically designed for general education. Furthermore, these colleges had great difficulty in procuring teachers who understood or were dedicated to general education."

Morse, Horace T., and Paul L. Dressel, eds. *General Education for Personal Maturity.* Dubuque, Iowa: William C. Brown Company, 1960.

This volume is unique in that it describes and analyzes a number of programs and courses offered as part of the general education program that are designed to assist students in meeting their personal problems. These "adjustment courses" are examined from three viewpoints: maturity in personal and social adjustment, maturity in preparation for marriage and family living, and maturity in the selection of a vocation. If education may be regarded as a quest for emotional and intellectual maturity, then all educational administrators involved in general education will find this book of great value. The focus of the volume is on *practical* courses in general education, designed to enhance the student's maturity—this is *not* a book on the philosophical quest for maturity.

President's Commission on Higher Education. *Higher Education for American Democracy, Volume I: Establishing the Goals.* Washington, D.C.: Government Printing Office, 1947. 103 pp.

Chapter 3 (pp. 47–66) propounds the thesis that general education is the basic ingredient for the education of free men, but that present (*circa* 1947) college programs fail to achieve this goal because "the unity of liberal education has been splintered by overspecialization." This chapter is perhaps the finest summary of general education found in any single volume. Not only are the needs, objectives, and methods of general education expounded, but the interrelationships between general and vocational education are dealt with as well.

Sexson, John A., and John W. Harbeson. *The New American College.* New York: Harper & Brothers, 1946. 312 pp.

A history of the experimental four-year public junior college, embracing the last two years of high school and the first two years of college, established in Pasadena, California. The program of general education employed, including practices, required courses, objectives, and timing, is found in Chapter 21 (pp. 242–251). It is noteworthy that the college relied on survey courses to meet the general education requirements.

Stickler, W. Hugh. *Organization and Administration of General Education.* Dubuque, Iowa: William C. Brown Company, 1951.

Provides a summary of the patterns of organization and administration of general education programs at twenty-two junior colleges and four colleges and universities (*circa* 1951). Summarizes the persistent problems plaguing the general education movement. Excellent for comparing the objectives and methods of achieving the objectives of diverse colleges, through the use of the general education curriculum. Includes much data on the results of these general education programs, as evaluated by the respective institutions.

Thomas, Russell. *The Search for a Common Learning: General Education, 1800–1960.* New York: McGraw-Hill Book Company, 1962. 324 pp.

Perhaps the definitive work on the origin of general education programs, their history, and the problems which confront them. Part I gives the historical background of the general education movement from 1800 to 1930. The focus is on the difficulties in reconciling the explosion of knowledge with the traditional college curriculum, and the gradual change in the concept of college education. Part II deals with the concept and practice of general education today, as carried out in eighteen representative institutions, each of which is treated in a separate chapter. Of special interest are the content of these general education programs and the specific objectives they are designed to fulfill. An indispensable work for those interested in general education.

Thornton, James W., Jr. *The Community Junior College.* New York: John Wiley & Sons, 1960. 300 pp.

Chapter 14 (pp. 197–214) discusses the practices in general education programs at community junior colleges and includes a survey of the objectives of courses in communications, social science, physical education, applied psychology, and preparation for marriage. Of particular value is the suggested program of general education for community college students (pp. 207–214).

Thornton, James W., Jr. "General Education." *The Public Junior College.* Fifty-fifth Yearbook of the National Society for the Study of Education, Part I. Chicago: The Society, 1956. Pp. 118–139.

A valuable overview of the general education programs in the public junior colleges, which explores the nature and scope of the general education programs, explains how the needs of the students are met by these programs, and notes the practices found in these programs (using examples). Concludes with an analysis of the deficiencies in these programs, and makes specific recommendations for correcting these deficiencies.

Ward, Phebe. *Terminal Education in the Junior College.* New York: Harper & Brothers, 1947. 282 pp.

Chapter 6, "Evaluating Terminal General-Education Programs" (pp. 214–227), delineates the methods and procedures developed at Wright Junior College in evaluating the effectiveness of the institution's general education program.

B. THE TRANSFER PROGRAM

Bird, Grace V. "Preparation for Advanced Study." *The Public Junior College.* Fifty-fifth Yearbook of the National Society for the Study of Education, Part I. Chicago: The Society, 1956. Pp. 77–93.

A report dealing with the transfer function of the junior college. Various studies available to the author indicate that junior college transfer students do about as well as native students in the junior and senior years. Some basic principles of sound relationships between junior and senior institutions are set forth to help effect a sound, efficient transfer program.

Blocker, Clyde E., Robert H. Plummer, and Richard C. Richardson, Jr. *The Two-Year College: A Social Synthesis.* Englewood Cliffs, N.J.: Prentice-Hall, 1965. 298 pp.

The transfer program is treated from a sociological viewpoint. Emphasis is placed on the consistency with which several factors, such as previous educational experience, family influences, and socio-economic level, affect the curricular choices of the students. Transferable credit is one of the expectations of the community college by the community, and hence is one of its major functions within its environment.

Bogue, Jesse P. *The Community College.* New York: McGraw-Hill Book Company, 1950. 390 pp.

Chapter 3 (pp. 45–76) delineates the basic functions of the community college, including the preparatory or transfer function. Cites Eells's study on transfer, based on the records of 2,080 graduates of junior colleges as reported from 319 senior colleges and universities, which indicates that transfer students do quite satisfactorily in junior and senior years, comparing favorably with native students.

Eells, Walter C. "The Junior College Transfer in the University." *The Junior College: Its Organization and Administration.* W. M. Proctor, ed. Stanford, Calif.: Stanford University Press, 1927. Pp. 171–187.

One of the first investigations to verify the success of the junior college in performing its transfer function.

Fields, Ralph R. *The Community College Movement.* New York: McGraw-Hill Book Company, 1962. 360 pp.

Suggests that the salvaging of students who were not eligible to enter senior college as freshmen, but after two years of successful work in the junior college are then eligible for transfer to a senior institution, is a community college function. Also gives specific examples of transfer curricula in several two-year institutions.

Hillway, Tyrus. *The American Two-Year College.* New York: Harper & Brothers, 1958. 276 pp.

Four functions—preparatory, popularizing, terminal, and guidance—were early assigned to the junior college; the preparatory function was listed as the most important. Among the present-day functions of the two-year college, the democratizing of higher education is the most important. The author emphasizes this greater opportunity for all to obtain collegiate experiences, including the opportunity to transfer to a senior institution at the end of the two-year program.

Holmes, Charles H. "The Transfer Student in the College of Arts." *Junior College Journal,* 31:456–461, April, 1961.

A comparative study was made between the transfer students of the four-year school group and of the two-year college group at the College of Liberal Arts in Syracuse University during the ten-year period 1946–1955. The general findings indicate that the two-year students who transferred had greater difficulty with academic adjustment than did the four-year transfers.

Kirk, Barbara A. "Comparison of Transfer Students by Source of Origin with Entering Students on the College Qualification Test." *Junior College Journal,* 29:218–221, December, 1958.

Comparison based on the standardization of the college qualification test developed by the Psychological Corporation. All entering students in the College of Letters and Science, including junior transfers, on the Berkeley campus of the University of California were given the test in the fall of 1956.

Knoell, Dorothy M., and Leland L. Medsker. *From Junior to Senior College: A National Study of the Transfer Student.* Washington, D.C.: American Council on Education, 1965. 102 pp.

A study involving over 10,000 students in 345 two-year colleges and 43 senior colleges and universities. It has implications for administrators, guidance counsellors, admissions officers, and parents. As the junior college assumes an increasing role in providing the first two years of college for more and more students, the findings of this study become increasingly important.

Koos, Leonard V. *The Junior College Movement.* Boston: Ginn & Company, 1925. 436 pp.

An old book of historic importance. Pages 92–99 provide some interesting considerations of the success of junior college graduates and the recognition of junior colleges by other higher educational institutions.

McDaniel, J. W., and Thomas Merson. "Selecting a College and a Program." *American Junior Colleges.* 6th ed. Edmund J. Gleazer, Jr., ed. Washington, D.C.: American Council on Education, 1963. Pp. 7–15.

Discusses transferability of junior college credit, success of students after transfer, characteristics of junior college students. Some illustrative programs of transfer are given; they are of two types: either a common liberal arts core with elective options, or a program embodying specializations which will be further developed in the upper divisions.

Martorana, S. V., and L. L. Williams. "Academic Success of Junior College Transfers at the State College of Washington." *Junior College Journal,* 24:402–415, March, 1954.

A comparative study of the achievements and the major fields of transfer and non-transfer groups at the State College of Washington, together with the interpretive data. The general conclusion reached was that when students are considered in groups, there is no significant difference between the academic success of the junior college transfer student and that of the native student.

Medsker, Leland L. *The Junior College: Progress and Prospect.* New York: McGraw-Hill Book Company, 1960. 367 pp.

Factors involved in transfer trends are pointed out in Chapter 4 (pp. 89–117). Several comparative studies are made between transfer and terminal functions. Chapter 5 (pp. 119–140) deals with the performance and retention of transfer students. On the whole the data seem to confirm that transfer students do quite well compared with native students. There is evidence to indicate that transfer students need greater preparation in the non-academic aspects of college life.

Neumaier, John J. "The Functions of the Junior College." *Junior College Journal,* 27:333–335, February, 1957.

Discusses four main functions ascribed to the junior college. The author suggests that transition from high school to college can be bridged with far greater ease in a junior college than in a larger university.

Sammartino, Peter, and Armand F. Burke. "Success of Junior Transfers in Eastern States." *Junior College Journal,* 17:307–310, March, 1947.

A report by the Transfer Study Committee of the Junior College Council of the Middle Atlantic States, covering transfer credit allowed; transfer students' major specialization in junior college; and marks earned in senior colleges by 262 junior college graduates, by regions.

Steggert, Francis X. "Terminal and University-Parallel Curricula in the Illinois Junior Colleges, 1951–1952." *College & University,* 28:204–209, January, 1953.

A study which concerns the twenty-six Illinois junior colleges (1952). Major outlines of the curricula are presented for both terminal and university-parallel functions. Most of the programs attempt to approximate the initial two years of the average senior college.

Stephens, Jean. "California Junior and Senior Colleges Work Together in Curriculum Planning." *Junior College Journal,* 30:147–148, November, 1959.

A successful example of curriculum planning between junior and senior colleges.

Thomas, Frank Waters. "The Functions of the Junior College." *The Junior College: Its Organization and Administration.* W. M. Proctor, ed. Stanford, Calif.: Stanford University Press, 1927. Pp. 11–25.

Designated (by Hillway) as one of the earliest efforts to give proper definition to the functions of the two-year college. The first defined function is that of preparing students for advanced work in the upper division of a four-year college or university.

Thornton, James W., Jr. *The Community Junior College.* New York: John Wiley & Sons, 1960. 300 pp.

Chapter 15 (pp. 215–235) is devoted to a discussion of transfer functions in the community colleges. Preparation for further study is identified as the "traditional task of the junior college."

C. THE VOCATIONAL-TECHNICAL PROGRAM

Birtwell, Helen C., comp. and ed. *Where to Find Vocational Training in New York City.* 17th ed. New York: Vocational Advisory Service, n.d. 316 pp.

Section I (pp. 3–154) presents "Schools and Subjects Taught," which consists of courses offered in trade schools, community colleges, and other institutions below a bachelor's degree level. Covered are such areas as accounting, construction, nursing, domestic arts, and drafting.

Brokenshire, John R., and others. *Directory of Occupation Centered Curriculums in California Junior Colleges and Schools for Adults.* (1964 Edition.) Sacramento, Calif.: California State Department of Education, 1964. 544 pp.

Planned originally as a tool for counsellors, this volume serves a wide variety of purposes. Occupational briefs are given in the general areas of agriculture, horticulture, and forestry; applied and graphic arts; business and management; trade and technical; health services; and other services. Accompanying each occupation is a chart indicating the colleges offering curriculums in that occupation. Pertinent information about the school or college, such as credits, degrees, certificates, school calendar, admission requirements, and tuition charges, is also given.

Corey, John. "North Carolina's New System of Vocational and Technical Education." *Phi Delta Kappan,* 46:383–387, April, 1965.

The comprehensive community college is demonstrated to be "North Carolina's answer to the need for vocational and technical education opportunities for youth beyond the high school." The author describes how two state systems—industrial centers and junior colleges—were merged to establish a new department of community colleges. Advantages of the new plan are described.

Harris, Norman C. "Redoubled Efforts and Dimly Seen Goals." *Phi Delta Kappan,* 46:360–365, April, 1965.

Parents, businessmen, industrialists, and legislators are seeking the answers to some very difficult questions about how best to prepare youth for jobs. Harris identifies the community junior college as the institution having "both the growth potential and the educational philosophy to serve as the capstone to the occupational education structure needed in the 1970's."

Harris, Norman C. *Technical Education in the Junior College: New Programs for New Jobs.* Washington, D.C.: American Association of Junior Colleges, 1964. 102 pp.

Describes occupational needs and sets forth procedures for establishing technical programs in the two-year colleges.

Harris, Norman C., and William R. Yencso. *Technical Education in Michigan Community Colleges.* Ann Arbor, Mich.: Office of Research Administration, The University of Michigan, 1965. 142 pp.

A detailed report of a study of the current status of collegiate technical programs in the state of Michigan, and of the feasibility of pre-technical curriculums in the high schools, sponsored by the State Board of Control for Vocational Education. The major finding of the study was the existence of a "disaster gap" for a large number of "middle level" high school graduates. Closer articulation between the high schools and the community colleges through the establishment of pre-technical programs is seen as the answer.

Henninger, G. Ross. *The Technical Institute in America.* New York: McGraw-Hill Book Company, 1959. 238 pp.

Report of the results of a national survey made in 1957 and 1958 for the purpose of revealing the present status and the future potential of technical institute education in America. The history of the technical institute is traced, its present status defined, and its future potential as well as its problems considered.

Johnson, B. Lamar. "Guidelines and Trends in Post-Secondary Vocational-Technical Education." *Phi Delta Kappan,* 46:376–380, April, 1965.

In developing guidelines for state programs for technical-vocational education, the emergence of the community college as a major, and perhaps dominant, avenue for technical-vocational education is indicated. The author points out eight trends in community college development that encourage and facilitate the development of such programs. The range of such programs is so wide that state systems of junior college education are imperative.

Occupational Criteria and Preparatory Curriculum Patterns in Technical Education Programs. Department of Health, Education, and Welfare, U.S. Office of Education. Washington, D.C.: Government Printing Office, 1962. 26 pp.

A report of considerable value in establishing sound objectives for technical education programs. Based on nationwide studies and research, the study presents educational concepts primarily from the standpoint of the two-year college preparatory program in occupational programs and the occupations to which they pertain.

Smith, Leo F., and Laurence Lipsett. *The Technical Institute.* New York: McGraw-Hill Book Company, 1956. 319 pp.

A comprehensive study of the technical institute in American higher education. Outlines techniques for organizing, administering, and evaluating technical institute programs.

Strong, Merle E., comp. *Curriculum Materials for Trade and Industrial Education, 1963.* Department of Health, Education, and Welfare, U.S. Office of Education. Washington, D.C.: Government Printing Office, 1964. 88 pp.

Readily available curriculum materials are listed, with brief annotations denoting the nature and content for those seeking specific information. Occupations covered range all the way from air conditioning and refrigeration to X-ray technician.

A Study of Technical Education in California. California State Department of Education, Bulletin, 28:7. Sacramento, Calif.: The Department, 1959. 122 pp.

Reviews a ten-year period of the development of technical education in the state and makes recommendations for future action.

Technical Education in the California Junior Colleges. Bureau of Industrial Education, California State Department of Education. Sacramento, Calif.: The Department, 1963. 22 pp.

Appraises the concepts, present programs, and future prospects for technical education in California and its junior colleges. Its purpose is "to encourage the further growth and development of technical education."

Venn, Grant. *Man, Education, and Work: Post Secondary Vocational and Technical Education.* Washington, D.C.: American Council on Education, 1964. 184 pp.

A study of the development of vocational and technical education, its modern imperatives, and the role of the federal government, with definition of issues and recommendations for action.

Vocational Education in the Junior College. State Committee on Vocational Education in the Junior College, California State Department of Education. Sacramento, Calif.: The Department, 1949. 88 pp.

The problem of providing junior college students with vocational guidance and training is the focus of this study. Growing out of four regional conferences and a number of regional workshops, it defines the problem; provides a checklist with a discussion of some items; presents several aspects of vocational education programs; and deals directly with the four major areas of vocational education: agricultural education, business education, home economics education, and industrial education.

Ward, Phebe. *Terminal Education in the Junior College.* New York: Harper & Brothers, 1947. 282 pp.

Extensive data on occupational-terminal curricula are presented from junior colleges in California. Procedures are formulated for developing such programs in the junior colleges on the basis of the reports.

D. NURSING EDUCATION

Anderson, Bernice E. *Nursing Education in Community Junior Colleges.* Philadelphia: J. B. Lippincott Company, 1966. 319 pp.

This publication presents a systematic appraisal of the development of associate degree nursing programs in community and junior colleges in New York, Texas, Florida, and California over a five-year period. Compiled by an experienced writer in the nursing field, this book fills a need for clear, readable guideposts for establishing these programs in new community junior colleges.

Brown, Esther Lucile. *Nursing for the Future: A Report Prepared for the National Nursing Council.* New York: Russell Sage Foundation, 1948. 198 pp.

An unusually well-qualified writer in the field of education for the professions appraises the requirements of the nursing profession as they reflect societal needs.

Buechel, J. F. Marvin. *Principles of Administration in Junior and Community College Education for Nursing.* New York: G. P. Putnam's Sons, 1956. 255 pp.

Report of a nationwide survey of community junior colleges offering programs for the education of student nurses. Current practices are appraised by Buechel, and then from the mass of data collected he formulates ten basic principles that describe desirable practices and may serve as guides for administrators in the community junior colleges with such programs or contemplating the establishing of such programs.

Frank, Sister Charles Marie, and Loretta E. Heidgerken, eds. *Perspectives in Nursing Education: Educational Patterns—Their Evolution and Characteristics.* Washington, D.C.: The Catholic University of America Press, 1963. 330 pp.

Presents an orderly view of nursing education in its academic setting. Part I presents a series of position papers; Part II summarizes the proceedings of yearly workshops at Catholic University since their inception in 1949.

Kinsinger, Robert E. *Education for Health Technicians—An Overview.* Washington: American Association of Junior Colleges, 1965. 35 pp.

A report intended "to provide an initial, brief introduction to an emerging and significant educational problem." That problem is the training of health service technicians to fill the needs of constantly evolving new health services growing directly out of scientific advancements. The author suggests that during the planning stage of curriculums for health technicians, the key is the educator—together with the employer and the technician—as he conducts cooperative planning projects and experiences to fill educational and practical needs. The author also pinpoints the critical need to identify and train outstanding technicians as teachers as a vital step in meeting this problem.

Lesnik, Milton J., and Bernice E. Anderson. *Legal Aspects of Nursing.* Philadelphia: J. B. Lippincott Company, 1947. 352 pp.

A monumental work on the legal aspects of the nursing profession, including their reflection in nursing as a profession; nursing programs of training; nursing course requirements; and many others.

Light, Israel. "Training for Health Occupations." *Junior College Journal,* 33:16–21, March, 1963.

Highlights the need for semiprofessional workers in health occupations and the implications of these needs for the two-year colleges.

Montag, Mildred L. *Community College Education for Nursing.* New York: McGraw-Hill Book Company, 1959. 457 pp.

The final report of the Cooperative Research Project in Junior and Community College Education for Nursing, covering a five-year period. It represents a report of the first major research project undertaken under the auspices of the Division of Nursing Education at Teachers College, Columbia University, under the directorship of the author. Part I describes the project, Part II evaluates the graduates of the program, and Part III presents conclusions and implications. The program reported is unique in several ways: it is a two-year program, in community and junior colleges, with students remaining under the jurisdiction of the college rather than the hospital during the entire period. Many other aspects are described, explored, and delineated in this definitive work on a now classic experiment in nursing education.

Montag, Mildred L. *The Education of Nursing Technicians.* New York: G. P. Putnam's Sons, 1951. 146 pp.

Reporting a study completed by the author as her doctoral project at Teachers College, Columbia University. The purpose of the study was to plan a program for the preparation of nurses with predominantly "technical" functions—as compared with the "professional" nurse. Guidelines are suggested for the training of professional nursing personnel to carry out such a program of technical nursing education. The author's suggested title for nurses between the professional and the practical nurse as "nursing technicians" was prophetic—it has become a commonly used designation today.

Nursing Education Facilities: Programing Considerations and Architectural Guide. Department of Health, Education, and Welfare, U.S. Public Health Service. Washington, D.C.: Government Printing Office, 1964. 88 pp.

Chapter 3 (pp. 18–27) deals with the associate degree nursing program, which is most often established as a department in a community college. The program is described together with the space needs for faculty, administration, supporting space, teaching space, and other space requirements. A budget exhibit is provided as an instructive example of the components and layout of a budget.

Nursing Education in Junior and Community Colleges. American Association of Junior Colleges, Cooperative Research Project in Junior and Community College Nursing Education, Columbia University and the National League for Nursing. New York: Teachers College, Columbia University, 1956. 76 pp.

Report of a conference held at Teachers College, Columbia University, sponsored jointly by the American Association of Junior Colleges, The National League for Nursing, and the Cooperative Research Project in Junior and Community College Nursing Education at Teachers College. The report consists of an examination of the historical, current, and future perspectives on nursing education in community junior colleges. It represents an invaluable source of information and guidelines for administrators contemplating the establishment of these programs in their colleges.

Pair, Nona Tiller, and Jo Eleanor Elliott. *One Road Toward Adequate Nursing Service*. Boulder, Colo.: Western Institute Commission for Higher Education, University East Campus, 1964. 16 pp.

This small booklet describes the planning of a nursing program in the junior college setting. It presents aids and guidelines for program planning.

Sindlinger, Walter E. "Experimentation in Education for Nursing at Orange County Community College." Doctor of Education Project Report, Teachers College, Columbia University, 1956. 235 pp. Typewritten.

A study of nursing education and the innovations involved in the establishing and developing of a two-year associate degree nursing program, under the guidance of the author, then academic dean at the community college.

E. BUSINESS EDUCATION

Chomitz, David L. *Business Education for Adults in the Junior College.* Monograph C-5. Cincinnati, Ohio: South-Western Publishing Company, 1957. 56 pp.

This monograph, a summary of portions of the doctoral project report of the author at Teachers College, is intended to provide information about the status of business education for adults in the junior colleges. The author identifies eighteen factors that characterize favorable conditions for the growth of adult business education in the junior colleges.

Crank, Doris H., and Floyd L. Crank. "New Perspectives for Business in the Junior College." *New Perspectives in Education for Business.* Washington, D.C.: National Business Education Association, 1963. Pp. 369–392.

Describes the increasing needs, the present status, and the future potential of business education in the junior colleges.

Gordon, Robert A., and James E. Howell. *Higher Education for Business.* New York: Columbia University Press, 1959. 491 pp.

A study of the development and status of business training in higher education. Suggests the need for reorganization and curricular reform.

Gratz, Jerre E. *Major Issues in Business Education.* Monograph 106. Cincinnati, Ohio: South-Western Publishing Company, 1962. 108 pp.

The findings in this monograph are taken from the more complete study submitted as the author's doctoral project at the

University of Houston. Although the issues presented are more properly directed to the secondary schools, almost every issue has some ramifications for junior colleges.

Kurtz, Margaret. "Technical Secretaries." *Junior College Journal,* 33:25–26, May, 1963.

Increased science education and the exposure to technical terminology and problems improves the secretary's usefulness to the employing industry.

McDivitt, W. L. "The Need for Junior Colleges." *Delta Pi Epsilon Journal,* 7:1–3, November, 1964.

Discusses the problem of academic excellence in the junior college and the dumping ground concept. This junior college president points toward the need for greater preparation for the world of work (business) to take care of the many students who find no place in the tightened and restricted college preparation curriculum. He states that "Sound programming can make tax producers out of potential tax consumers . . . ."

McGrath, James J., and Rosalind H. Solon. "The Role of the Advisory Commission in the Accounting Curriculum of a Community College." *Delta Pi Epsilon Journal,* 7:4–12, November, 1964.

One of the historic strengths of American education has been its control and advisement by lay personnel in the community. The authors indicate the need for a lay advisory committee to guide a technical department in a community college. Some of the areas in which an advisory committee can be helpful are: planning and scope of the curriculum, providing instructional materials, evaluation and revision of the curriculum, recruitment of students and teachers, and interpreting the curriculum to the public.

Nanassy, Louis C., ed. *Business Education Index, 1964.* Vol. 25. Compiled yearly by Delta Pi Epsilon. New York: McGraw-Hill Book Company, 1965. 70 pp.

An index of business education articles listed alphabetically in an author-and-subject listing that is compiled from a selected list of periodicals and yearbooks published during the year. Delta Pi Epsilon is the national honorary graduate fraternity in business education.

Pierson, Frank C., and others. *The Education of American Businessmen.* New York: McGraw-Hill Book Company, 1959. 740 pp.

While the major concern in this volume is the status of the four-year and graduate programs in business administration, Chapter 23 is concerned with the junior college business program.

Planning and Equipping Business Education Classrooms. Bureau of Business Education, California State Department of Education. Sacramento, Calif.: The Department, 1961. 33 pp.

While this booklet deals primarily with the planning of facilities, it does emphasize the important relationships that exist between the curriculum on the one hand and the facilities and personnel requirements on the other.

F. AUTOMATION AND TELEVISION

Cooper, W. L. "Uses of Tapes, Language Laboratory, and Teaching Teams at the J. Sterling Morton High School and Junior College." *Bulletin* of the National Association of Secondary-School Principals, 44:233–243, January, 1960.

Describes four projects concerned with the use of tapes, the use of language laboratory, and with the team-teaching approach at the J. Sterling Morton High School and Junior College (Cicero, Illinois) during the autumn semester of the 1958–59 school year. The team-teaching approach was related to the teaching of American history and American literature.

Design for ETV: Planning for Schools with Television. Prepared by Dave Chapman, Inc., Industrial Design for Educational Facilities Laboratories. New York: Educational Facilities Laboratories, 1960. 96 pp.

Not concerned directly with the community college, nevertheless this study is valuable to all levels of the educational enterprise. The elements that affect the educational program are presented; the importance of relationships of size, group quality, and height of teaching image to group size, viewing angles, and distances are described. Methods of design for educational facilities are explored in relation to function.

Erickson, Clifford G., and Hymen M. Chausow. *Chicago's TV College: Final Report of a Three-Year Experiment of the Chicago City Junior College in Offering College Courses for Credit Via Open Circuit Television.* Chicago: Chicago City Junior College, 1960. 98 pp.

Presents a comprehensive resumé of the first three years of operation of the open-circuit instructional program in terms of courses, instructional materials, instructors, enrollments, examinations, etc. General conclusions reached were that open-circuit television instruction can be used effectively in a large metropolitan community; that a large, serious, and able student body can be reached in this manner; that instruction can be effectively given without compromising quality; and that credits thus earned are recognized by many senior colleges and accrediting agencies.

Erickson, Clifford G., Hymen M. Chausow, and James J. Zigerell. *Eight Years of TV College: A Fourth Report.* Chicago: Chicago Board of Education and the Chicago City Junior College, 1964. 40 pp.

Reviews the expanded activities of TV College to-date. Among these activities are joint television courses offered with Chicago Teachers College, to provide in-service instruction for teachers; special programs instituted for partially handicapped students and shut-ins; pilot studies in accelerated courses for gifted students; and a program of study via open-circuit television for prison inmates leading to the associate in arts degree. Also described are cost factors, teacher recruitment, enrollment trends, and other factors pertinent to the TV College.

Florida Education, 42:1–48 (entire issue), October, 1964.

This issue of the monthly organ of the Florida Education Association presents an excellent profile of educational television in that state. Various articles trace the history of ETV in the state and deal with developments in all aspects of the development, production, and evaluation of educational television in Florida.

Price, Wilson T., and Raymond A. Barnett. "Beginning Computer Education." *Junior College Journal*, 34:19–23, September, 1963.

Report of a survey of computer programs in California junior colleges. Gives lists of California junior colleges having computers, the types, programs used, and auxiliary equipment.

Technical Education Program Series No. 4, Electronic Data Processing—I: A Suggested 2-Year Post High School Curriculum for Computer Programers and Business Applications Analysts. Department of Health, Education, and Welfare, U.S. Office of Education. Washington, D.C.: Government Printing Office, 1963. 49 pp.

Designed as a guide for planning preparatory programs and extension courses for employed persons. The curriculum presented here is designed to provide the maximum specialization achievable in a two-year program. It includes an introduction to the field, computer programing, mechanics of data processing, mathematics and communications skills, and suggestions for extensive individual projects and group assignments.

G. CURRICULUM DEVELOPMENT

Britton, Ernest R. "Making the Community Self Survey Study." *Bulletin* of the National Association of Secondary-School Principals, 37:385–392, April, 1953.

Sets forth steps and principles to be followed in making a community survey and illustrates the advantages for the curriculum development program which result.

Brunner, Ken August. *Guide to Organized Occupational Curriculums in Higher Education.* Washington, D.C.: Government Printing Office, 1965. 108 pp.

This survey by the Office of Education reveals that organized occupational programs of at least one but less than four years in length existed in 879 institutions of higher education in the United States. An increase in enrollment of 10.8 per cent from 1960 to 1962, there being in the latter year 274,725 students in technical or semiprofessional curriculums, is also noted. The five leading organized occupational curriculum areas in terms of enrollees were business and commerce, electrical technology, health service, education, and mechanical technology. Institutional data about these programs are presented.

Dressel, Paul L. *The Undergraduate Curriculum in Higher Education.* Washington, D.C.: Center for Applied Research in Education, 1963. 110 pp.

The author analyzes the nature of, and the assumptions underlying, present curriculums and offers suggestions for their reform. Only indirect pertinence to junior colleges.

Eells, Walter C. *Why Junior College Terminal Education?* Washington, D.C.: American Association of Junior Colleges, 1941. 365 pp.

The then Executive Secretary of the AAJC and the Commission on Junior College Terminal Education presents fundamental reasons for the importance of terminal education in the junior colleges. Chapters 2 and 3 contain an overview of the social, economic, and educational factors that have set the stage for the present movement (1941).

Fields, Ralph R. *The Community College Movement.* New York: McGraw-Hill Book Company, 1962. 360 pp.

Chapters 3 (pp. 63–99) and 10 (pp. 286–306) set forth the variety and scope of the vocational, technical, terminal programs in the community colleges. Examples of curricular development within specific community colleges are given.

Fields, Ralph R. "Curriculum Development in Professional Education." *The Journal of the American Dental Hygienists' Association,* 40:12–20, First Quarter, 1966.

Working from some twenty years' experience in curriculum and instruction problems in a professional school of education, Fields attacks the problem of curriculum development by asking some very basic (difficult) questions: What are our purposes? What will we teach? How will we organize the curriculum? He answers his questions with a set of nine principles that, while offering no permanent solutions, may serve as guidelines to aid in meeting the "continuous challenge" of curriculum development.

General Education. Fifty-first Yearbook of the National Society for the Study of Education, Part I. Chicago: The Society, 1952. 377 pp.

A comprehensive treatment of the theory and practice of general education in American higher education.

Gross, Richard E., and David M. Maynard. "Junior College Social Science Offerings Reflect Curricular Problems." *Junior College Journal,* 33:210–215, December, 1962.

Examines problems of gaps, duplications, and articulation between high school and junior college social sciences. Stresses need for study of other lands.

Harris, Norman C. *Curriculum Development for Hawaii's Community Colleges with Emphasis on Occupational Education.* Honolulu: Community College System, University of Hawaii, 1965. 110 pp.

Under the Community College Act of 1964, the existing technical schools are intended to be incorporated into the community college system. To make this transition efficiently, the author hereby sets forth the results of a study of the present situation and changes recommended—a very precise presentation of the entire plan for community college development in Hawaii. Of special interest is the appendix, containing sample instruments for community surveys.

Harris, Norman C. "A Special Role in Engineering Education." *Junior College Journal,* 33:8–12, April, 1963.

Discusses selection of students and guidance and curriculum considerations in two-year college transfer programs in engineering.

Johnson, B. Lamar. *General Education in Action: A Report of the California Study of General Education in the Junior College.* Washington, D.C.: American Council on Education, 1952. 409 pp.

Describes general education practices in California public junior colleges, based on a 14-month study of 57 institutions. Includes chapters on needs for and goals of general education, and also addresses itself to the major subject areas within such a program.

Mayhew, Lewis B., ed. *General Education: An Account and Appraisal.* New York: Harper & Brothers, 1960. 212 pp.

A guide for college faculties in clarifying aims, improving curriculum, and strengthening teaching in general education programs.

Meister, Morris, and Abraham Tauber. "Experiments in Expanding Educational Opportunity for the Disadvantaged." *Phi Delta Kappan,* 56:340–342, March, 1965.

Two programs at the Bronx (New York) Community College designed to provide higher educational opportunities for the underprivileged are described by the president and dean. "Operation Second Chance," begun in 1959 with Ford Foundation help, proved that "thousands of high school graduates now rejected by colleges could, with special treatment and appropriate programs, profit significantly from higher education." The College Discovery Program of the City University of New York is giving further evidence at Bronx Community College that many students who would be rejected for college admission by usual standards can succeed when given the opportunity.

This article exemplifies a commendable leadership role by an urban community college in extending higher educational opportunities to the underprivileged.

Nall, Alfred W. "What About 'Terminal' General Education in the Junior Colleges?" *Junior College Journal,* 33:20–24, September, 1962.

A role for the junior colleges in providing for "terminal" general education is presented. Such general education has the following distinctive characteristics: (1) it is designed to fit the characteristics of a specified group of students; (2) it includes knowledge, skills, and practice for living in a democratic society; (3) it provides a particularly pertinent course content; (4) it utilizes the most appropriate study materials; (5) it applies the most effective methods of instruction; (6) it places special emphasis on artistry in teaching; and (7) it diversifies evaluation of student growth and achievement.

Passow, A. Harry, ed. *Curriculum Crossroads.* New York: Teachers College Press, Teachers College, Columbia University, 1962. 123 pp.

Report of a curriculum conference that concerned itself with many aspects of curriculum development, including assessing curriculum proposals, decision-making and the teacher, and the disciplines as curriculum content.

Rushing, Joe B. "Your Community Can Help." *Junior College Journal,* 33:8–10, May, 1963.

The author points out advantages of advisory committees to colleges and presents some guidelines for establishing these committees.

Thomas, Russell. *The Search for a Common Learning: General Education, 1800–1960.* New York: McGraw-Hill Book Company, 1962. 324 pp.

A study of the historical background and development of general education and an exploration of the contemporary situation.

Vaccaro, Louis C. "The Manpower Development and Training Act and the Community College." *Junior College Journal,* 34:21–23, November, 1963.

The author points out that the very nature of the act suggests that it covers the total spectrum of vocational and/or occupational skills; hence it is directly related to the transfer, terminal, community service, and guidance functions of the community college.

Venn, Grant. *Man, Education, and Work: Post Secondary Vocational and Technical Education.* Washington, D.C.: American Council on Education, 1964. 184 pp.

A study of the development of vocational and technical education, its modern imperatives, and the role of the federal government, with definition of issues and recommendations for implementation.

Ward, Phebe. *Terminal Education in the Junior College.* New York: Harper & Brothers, 1947. 282 pp.

Reports the principles and practices of terminal education as disclosed by analysis of junior college programs over the nation, and of community colleges in California. Still serves as a blueprint for vocational-terminal curriculum development.

Wilcox, Edward T. "The New Curriculum." *Junior College Journal,* 33:16–18, February, 1963.

A thought-provoking article that probes the present-day flexibility of the curriculum. The author suggests that in spite of this far-reaching flexibility, the "new curriculum" will "maintain without any inconsistency, a cohesive program that can be taken without embarrassment by students who wish a terminal degree at the end of two or of four years."

H. ADULT AND CONTINUING EDUCATION

Bogue, Jesse P. "Adult Education in the Community College." *The Community College.* New York: McGraw-Hill Book Company, 1950. Pp. 207–237.

Adult education is inescapable for the colleges that profess to serve the entire community. Adult education cannot be properly conceived as an emergency program, or as an attempt to provide for upgrading workers, or to take up slack of increasing leisure time. It is basic to the essential progress of society itself, for democratic citizenship, sound individualism, and humanism. Basic to success in adult education is the sense of freedom that must pervade the program in every respect.

Burch, Glenn. *Challenge to the University: An Inquiry into the University's Responsibility for Adult Education.* Chicago: Center for the Study of Liberal Education for Adults, 1961. 79 pp.

While not dealing with the community junior college as such, this booklet presents many pertinent ideas that are applicable to two-year institutions. The author divides the public service functions—as distinct from regular teaching functions—into three areas: extension service, educational services, and continuing education.

Carter, Robert P. "The Community College: Its Opportunity in Leisure Education." Doctor of Education Project Report, Teachers College, Columbia University, 1957. 381 pp. Typewritten.

This work addresses itself to a definition of "leisure education" and delineates the role of the community college in providing it.

Dickerman, Watson. "What is This Continuing Education?" *Adult Education,* 15:3–8, Autumn, 1964.

The author highlights the idea of continuing. He emphasizes the idea that continuing education is necessary for survival.

Hillway, Tyrus. "Cooperative and Adult Education." *The American Two-Year College.* New York: Harper & Brothers, 1958. Pp. 117–141.

States advantages, values, needs for, and the varieties of adult and cooperative education.

Houle, Cyril O. *Major Trends in Higher Adult Education.* Chicago: Center for the Study of Liberal Education for Adults, 1959. 45 pp.

Describes how adult education is carried out in our various institutions. Details four reasons why community colleges are so important in the spread of adult education: (1) they are geographically dispersed throughout the country; (2) adult education has been an integral part of community college education from the beginning; (3) the community college is in essence a teaching unit; and (4) in many places community colleges have a natural and easy means of financing adult education. The community college is the institution through which large numbers of people can be reached; the author feels the leaders are creative.

Kaplan, Abbot, ed. "Continuing Education." *Journal of Higher Education,* 35:466–468, November, 1964.

Describes the Bell Telephone experiment of sending company executives to a ten-month institute at the University of Pennsylvania. The result of the experiment indicated that, in the long run, continuous exposure to education and the constant stimulus and challenge of abstract ideas and concepts sharpen the mind and develop the imagination.

Kempfer, Homer H. "The Community College and Adult Education." *Adult Education Bulletin,* 14:166–172, August, 1950.

The article gives a definition of the term "Community College" and examines the various educational approaches upon which the community college might draw in ascertaining needs upon which the educational programs for adults can be based.

Knowles, Malcolm. "The Future of Adult Education." *The Adult Education Movement in the United States.* New York: Holt, Rinehart and Winston, 1962. Pp. 269–280.

Several trends are apparent: adult education will continue to grow, resources and facilities will gradually expand, curriculum and methodology will become increasingly differentiated from those designated for children and youth, rapid expansion in the body of knowledge about education of adults will take place, and the role of adult education will be different from that of other levels of education. The purpose of adult education will be to emphasize learning to learn rather than transmission of knowledge.

Koch, Moses S., and Saul E. Lilienstein. "Community College Attracts the Aging." *Junior College Journal,* 35:26–27, October, 1964.

Essex Community College, in Maryland, held a day of classes for the aging. Results were surprising: while about 45 were expected, over 100 attended. This article discusses an interesting experiment for intellectually oriented senior citizens in a community college.

Leopold, Alice K. "The Junior College Must Provide Appropriate Educational Programs for Women." *Junior College Journal,* 31:519–520, May, 1961.

The author, formerly Assistant to the Secretary of Labor, points out that the junior college has a very real part to play in the education of women through the great diversity of its courses and offerings, and because of its emphasis on part-time courses for workers and wives.

Martorana, S. V. "Problems in Adult Education in the Junior College." *Junior College Journal,* 18:115–123, November, 1947.

Deals with problems in starting adult education programs. A checklist was sent to all junior colleges listed by the American Association of Junior Colleges. Results of the survey: 79 per cent had difficulties coordinating program with those of other agencies; 76 per cent had difficulty integrating program with other units in school system; and 93 per cent had difficulty developing the criteria to determine need for courses.

Martorana, S. V. "Status of Adult Education in Junior Colleges." *Junior College Journal,* 18:322–331, February, 1948.

Summarizes the results of a study of the number and types of junior colleges offering programs for adults. Covers enrollments in these institutions and types of programs offered.

Medsker, Leland L. "An Educational Program with Many Purposes." *The Junior College: Progress and Prospect.* New York: McGraw-Hill Book Company, 1960. Pp. 51–88.

Community college adult education should *not* be just the offering of a series of non-credit, unrelated courses that have been developed through speculation. Many times these courses pertain primarily to crafts, recreation, or vocational skills. Medsker feels that the college soon becomes a center of attraction for adults. He also believes both day and evening classes should be taught for adults. In short, adult education has many facets and is woven into the general pattern of a community-centered institution.

Mosley, John W. "Adult Education in the Community College." *Junior College Journal,* 20:75–81, October, 1949.

The community college should perform two functions in its adult education programs: (1) direct work of institutions so that it will "*supplement*" the work of other agencies, thereby providing community service, and (2) "*exert* leadership" by offering outstanding adult education programs.

Petersen, Renee, and William Petersen. *University Adult Education.* New York: Harper & Brothers, 1960. 288 pp.

Surveys the extension and adult education services of many colleges and universities. Indicates what is wrong in adult education and emphasizes the basic principles, policies, and procedures that are most likely to bring about good adult education in our institutions of higher education.

Sheats, Paul H., Clarence D. Jayne, and Ralph B. Spence. *Adult Education: The Community Approach.* New York: The Dryden Press, 1953. 530 pp.

The central theme is that of continuing education, which the authors believe is essential in maintaining our democratic way of life. The central focus of the adult program is the community. Many examples of programs under way in a variety of agencies are given.

Thornton, James W., Jr. "The Curriculum: Adult Education." *The Community Junior College.* New York: John Wiley & Sons, 1960. Pp. 236–251.

The community college accepts the individual purposes of its adult students. In addition, it realizes its obligation to society in seeking solutions to social problems. Among the social considerations that influence junior colleges in providing adult education are: rapid increase in knowledge, demands of enlightened citizenship, and cultural deprivation.

I. COMMUNITY DEVELOPMENT

Barnes, J. B. "The Community College's Newest Obligation." *Junior College Journal,* 28:247–250, January, 1958.

Six well-known characteristics of the community college are mentioned, characteristics that are well established and which have been thoroughly discussed. The author propounds a new obligation—that of community development. Several reasons are given why the community college is uniquely adapted to help solve community problems.

Biddle, William W. *Community Development Process: The Rediscovery of Local Initiative.* New York: Holt, Rinehart and Winston, 1965. 334 pp.

A series of terms, such as "education and community development," are defined. The author states a philosophy of community development, gives examples of such developments, and describes the process of community development. Written from a psychological-sociological-anthropological point of view.

Education for Better Living: The Role of the School in Community Improvement. Bulletin, 1956, No. 9. Yearbook on Education Around the World. Department of Health, Education, and Welfare, U.S. Office of Education. Washington, D.C.: Government Printing Office, 1957. 339 pp.

Group accounts by authors from around the world. Covers the school, adult education, etc. A world-wide trend is shown in relating education to needs of the community and helping communities improve themselves through education.

Essert, Paul L. "The Criteria Applied to Adult Study for Community Development." *Creative Leadership of Adult Education.* Englewood Cliffs, N.J.: Prentice-Hall, 1955. Pp. 91–199.

Details principles for community development. Gives examples of various types of community development programs and describes the process of community development. Indicates the unique role of the community college in community planning and development.

Fields, Ralph R. "The Program Defined and Implemented." *The Public Junior College.* Fifty-fifth Yearbook of the National Society for the Study of Education. Chicago: The Society, 1956. Pp. 163–190.

Discusses the instructional program: what it is, how it is conceived, and how it is implemented. Alludes to the fact that community service is a very important part of community college programs.

Harrington, John H. "Blueprint for Developing Community College Curriculums." *Junior College Journal,* 22:193–200, December, 1951.

Outlines and discusses the procedures that evolved in one community college in developing a program for adults in response to a specific and strong demand from community agencies. Traces the procedures from first awareness of demand to follow-up results.

Kempfer, Homer H. "Adult Education in the Community College." *Junior College Journal,* 21:18–25, September, 1950.

Describes adult education programs in community colleges. A section of the article deals with the "educational influence of the community college." It should be directed through community organizations; thus it can extend education to community. Whether through training sessions for community leaders, consultation services, or coordinating efforts, or by providing equipment and facilities, community colleges can enrich the education received by members of the community. Projects should develop under bilateral leadership. Maximum participation by the community being served is the cardinal principle involved.

Moore, James W., and J. William Rioux. "Two Challenges of the Economic Opportunity Act." *Junior College Journal,* 35:17–18, March, 1965.

How community colleges can make use of the Economic Opportunity Act is the theme. Both Title I-C and Title II contain programs of special interest to community colleges. Title II should be of interest to adult educators, because it has provisions for a community action program.

Reynolds, James W. "Community Services." *The Public Junior College.* Fifty-fifth Yearbook of the National Society for the Study of Education, Part I. Chicago: The Society, 1956. Pp. 140–160.

This article classifies the range of possible community services discussed in other studies into the following categories: mutual aid for meeting community college needs, community study and research problems, public affairs education, community development, and community use of school plant.

Rubin, Max J. "Responsible Community Leadership." *New York State Education,* 52:10–11+, December, 1964.

Deals with the subject of integration. The author states that there must be close cooperation between community leadership and educational leadership; the community and the school must work together to solve mutual problems.

The Yearbook Committee, National Society for the Study of Education. "The Role of the Public Junior College." *The Public Junior College.* Fifty-fifth Yearbook of the National Society for the Study of Education, Part I. Chicago: The Society, 1956. Pp. 64–74.

Discusses purposes of the junior college, including community service. The Committee states that, in addition to providing both credit and non-credit courses, the community college should take the lead in improving community activities and services.

VI. Community Junior College Personnel

A. ADMINISTRATIVE PERSONNEL

Blocker, Clyde E., and Henry A. Campbell. *Attitudes of Administrators toward the Administrative Organization of Public Junior Colleges in Seven States.* Austin, Texas: The authors, 1962. 41 pp.

Considering the administrative organization of the junior college as one index of its status, the authors examined the concepts and attitudes that two-year-college administrators have regarding the advantages or disadvantages of the various organizational structures of junior colleges. They conclude from the data that the administrative structure of the junior college must be appropriate to the needs of the community that supports it; hence there probably is no "best" organization for a majority of the colleges.

Blocker, Clyde E., and Robert H. McCabe. *Relationships between the Informal Organization and the Curriculum in Six Junior Colleges.* Austin, Texas: The authors, 1964. 125 pp. Mimeographed.

The present report is "the outgrowth of one of five studies of the informal organizations of seventeen community colleges and one four-year college" through sociometric analysis of the influence structures. Its purpose is to develop a design for analyzing the influence structure of school staffs in relation to curriculum matters. The study was conducted in six southwestern schools.

Blocker, Clyde E., Robert H. McCabe, and Albert J. Prendergast. *A Method for the Sociometric Analysis of the Informal Organization within Large Work Groups.* Austin, Texas: The authors, 1964. 53 pp.

This report is one of several exploring the informal organizations within institutions of higher learning. Its purpose is to provide a body of empirical data to assist administrators in grasping the significance of group dynamics and their implications for effective decision-making. The authors converted their data into a computer program. The method thus developed has been tested in seventeen junior colleges, and several dissertations have been written in the junior college field using the method.

Fitch, Naomi. *Comparative Study of Faculty Association Functions in California Junior Colleges.* Project Report, Kellogg Leadership Program, University of California, Summer, 1964. Berkeley, Calif.: University of California, Berkeley, 1964. 138 pp.

A survey of the faculty associations in fifty-three California junior colleges, indicating a quite rapid trend toward greater faculty participation in the formulation of institutional policies. Also demonstrates that the pattern of relationships between the faculty association and faculty senates as they are formed shows wide variation and points up the need for more clearly identified areas of responsibility and duties.

Hungate, Thad L. *Management in Higher Education.* New York: Teachers College Press, Teachers College, Columbia University, 1964. 348 pp.

This is undoubtedly the best delineation of the duties and responsibilities of administrative officers in educational institutions to be found anywhere. A clear, concise, and well-written work; the philosophy presented for the management of higher educational institutions is timely and sound. This book is "must" reading for all administrators in higher education.

Priest, Bill J. "Selecting a College President." *Junior College Journal,* 35:5–7, April, 1965.

The most important function of the junior college board of trustees is the selection of the college president, for the development of the college for years to come will undoubtedly depend on the wisdom of the choice. The chairman of the Subcommittee on Appropriate AAJC Placement Services of the Commission on Administration sets forth the normal steps to be taken in choosing a college president, together with some enrichment ideas that might facilitate the process.

Schultz, Raymond E. *Administrators for America's Junior Colleges: Predictions of Need 1965–1980.* Washington, D.C.: American Association of Junior Colleges, 1965. 28 pp.

Several startling predictions are made as the result of a nation-wide survey of junior colleges. Among them: there will be a need for almost 3,000 new administrators over the next 15 years; less than half of the junior college presidents hold an earned doctorate; and more than three-fourths of the private junior college presidents are over 53 years of age. These findings highlight two critical problems: what will be the source of these administrators? and what qualifications should they possess?

Schultz, Raymond E. "Changing Profile of the Junior College President." *Junior College Journal,* 36:8–13, October, 1965.

Presents additional information on new junior college presidents as a result of a nationwide survey. Findings indicate that most of the recently appointed presidents are older, have greater experience, and are better educated than their colleagues. Probably the most interesting finding is that older men are being chosen as new college presidents—as more and more new presidents are needed, just the opposite would seem to be logical. The rate at which such presidents are being attracted to other positions is on the increase.

"Symposium: Need for Administrative Leadership in Junior Colleges." *Journal of Secondary Education,* 36:29–64, January, 1961.

Recognizing the critical need for competently trained administrators in the many new junior colleges, the W. K. Kellogg

Foundation provided a substantial grant to selected universities to explore the problem. This report reviews the proceedings of the first institute organized at UCLA under the program, July 6–8, 1960. Six recognized leaders in higher education treat administrative leadership from various viewpoints. The series of papers is also published separately in a booklet by the University of California Junior College Leadership Program.

B. INSTRUCTIONAL PERSONNEL

Bard, Harry. "Teaching at the Junior College Level: Some Guideposts for the Improvement of Instruction." *Junior College Journal,* 32:437–440, April, 1962.

The president of the Baltimore Junior College provides a list of guidelines for the junior college instructor wishing to improve his teaching. They are solid axioms for all who would profess to teach others.

Community College Research Symposium: The Community College Faculty and Staff. Proceedings of a symposium held in Seattle, Washington, February 8–9, 1963. Olympia, Wash.: State Superintendent of Public Instruction, 1963. Pp. 98–131.

Two research papers on the community college faculty and a discussion of each are presented. Such items as preparation, degrees held, types of educational preparation, amount and type of experience, salary ranges, and teaching loads are dealt with. The most clearly evolving problem seemed to be the conflict arising from attempts to make competence and salaries closer to those enjoyed by senior institutions while at the same time attempting to retain the spark of individuality and independence indicative of community college vitality. Each research paper includes an excellent bibliography.

"Does it Pay to Teach in College?" *NEA Research Bulletin,* 38:35–40, May, 1960.

Findings in this report indicate that, while there are great variations from one section of the country to another, generally the best of the junior college teaching salaries compare favorably with the salaries paid in a great many senior institutions. Gives statistics on high, low, and average salary for junior and senior institutions, and for men and women in different sections of the country.

Eurich, Alvin C. "Staffing Junior Colleges." *Junior College Journal,* 33:8–12, March, 1963.

As the teacher shortage intensifies, administrators of junior colleges need to consider two basic problems: how can a larger share of the ablest teachers be attracted to junior colleges, and how can the available teaching talent be used more effectively? In a paper originally given at the 1963 AAJC Convention, Eurich proceeds to offer profound thoughts on ways these two problems can be faced. He especially emphasizes the better utilization of the faculty members by the full use of the results of modern innovations and techniques.

Hendrix, Vernon L. "Relationships Between Personnel Policies and Faculty Personality Characteristics in Public Junior Colleges." *California Journal of Educational Research,* 15:34–43, January, 1964.

The literature of personnel administration assumes that the desirability of tenure, rank, and evaluation is related to an improvement in the institution. "Since it is usually claimed that this is done by attracting and retaining 'good' faculty members, it appears reasonable to deduce that the faculties in colleges with or without certain policies should differ." The writer reports the results of his research on personality factors in Texas public junior college faculties.

Kuhns, Eileen P. "Part-Time Faculty." *Junior College Journal,* 33:8–12, January, 1963.

Part-time instructors, who teach in the evening division of our junior colleges, bring a special interest and zeal to the classroom. Often they practice highly specialized skills in business and the professions during the day—the same skills in which they give instruction in the evening classroom. The author presents many reasons why the part-time instructor is a vitalizing influence.

Especially noteworthy is the reference to retired people who can bring to the classroom an entire lifetime of experience and expertise in a specialized field.

Maul, Ray C. "Are Junior College Salaries Competitive?" *Junior College Journal*, 34:20–23, March, 1964.

The staffing problems of the junior colleges rest upon three main questions: (1) How many new teachers must be recruited each year? (2) Will these new teachers be adequately prepared? (3) What salaries will be necessary to attract and hold these teachers in the numbers needed? The author presents statistics on average, high, and low salary ranges which indicate that there is unusually wide variation in geographic areas. Many other facts are given.

Merson, Thomas B., comp. *Preparation of Junior College Instructors: Part II, Programs of Junior College Teacher Education in Selected Colleges and Universities.* Washington, D.C.: American Association of Junior Colleges, 1963. Not consecutively paginated. Mimeographed.

The results of a request letter sent to twenty colleges and universities having preparatory programs for junior college teachers; the letters received in reply are presented in the first section of this report. The second section describes a number of college and university training programs for the preparation of junior college technical instructors, compiled by Dr. Norman Harris of the University of Michigan.

Preparation of Junior College Instructors: Part III, Recommendations From Representative Junior College Staffs. Washington, D.C.: American Association of Junior Colleges, 1963. Unpaged. Mimeographed.

This publication presents the responses of selected junior colleges to a letter asking them to describe abilities, competencies, and skills required, in their experience, by junior college instructors and their recommendations for program elements whereby these attributes can be developed. It is the third document resulting from a major program on instructor recruitment, preparation, and utilization undertaken by the American Association of Junior Colleges.

Priest, Bill J. "Faculty-Administrator Relationships." *Junior College Journal,* 34:4–8, March, 1964.

It once was true that "board members make policy, administrators administrate, and teachers teach." But this is a dictum that is being belligerently challenged today in many junior colleges across the country, and especially in California. The rise of the faculty senate, the appearance of numerous teachers' organizations, and many other indications verify this fact. The president of the American River Junior College in California goes on to raise many thought-provoking ideas as a result of these movements.

Siehr, Hugo E., John X. Jamrich, and Karl T. Hereford. *Problems of New Faculty Members in Community Colleges.* Washington, D.C.: American Association of Junior Colleges, 1963. 72 pp.

Report on the findings of a study of problems of new community college faculty members, administrative practices that were helpful in alleviating these problems, and suggestions for improvement of the orientation of new faculty members as a result.

Stone, James C., and Dale Tillery. *The Preparation of Teachers for the Junior Colleges.* Washington, D.C.: American Association of Junior Colleges, 1963. 26 pp. Mimeographed.

A position paper prepared for the AAJC by faculty members at the School of Education of the University of California, Berkeley. Focuses on challenges and frustrations facing the junior colleges, with special emphasis on ways of accelerating the preparation of future teachers for the two-year institutions. It represents Part I of a three-part series on the recruitment, preparation, and utilization of junior college instructors undertaken by the American Association of Junior Colleges.

C. ACADEMIC RANK

Blocker, Clyde E., and Wendell Wolfe. "Academic Rank in Two-Year Colleges." *Junior College Journal,* 35:21–25, December, 1964.

This report indicates that: (1) there is an accelerating trend toward the use of faculty ranks in junior colleges; (2) administrators seem to be prime motivators for the adoption of ranking; (3) ranking is much more widespread in the Middle Atlantic and New England states than in other sections of the United States; and (4) ranking is closely associated with ". . . strong desire for the acquisition of the symbols of the academic caste system in higher education."

Bokelman, W. Robert, and Louis A. D'Amico. "The Distribution of Faculty Ranks by Institutional Type, Size, and Control, 1960–61." *AAUP Bulletin,* 47:242–246, September, 1961.

Comparisons of rank distributions by size and type of institution, including medical and other graduate schools. The information upon which the article is based suggests that there is a correlation between size and type of institution and rank—large public institutions have the greatest percentage of full professors; assistant professors and instructors in private institutions represent a greater percentage of the faculty than in public institutions; and full professor has the highest percentage representation in medical and graduate schools.

Eells, Walter Crosby. "Distribution of Instructional Ranks." *Journal of Higher Education,* 33:47–49, January, 1962.

A brief presentation of the relative numbers of individuals holding the various academic ranks at institutions of higher education.

Freiberger, Helenes T., and W. H. Crawford. "Junior College Academic Rank and Title." *Junior College Journal,* 33:89–92, October, 1962.

There is no longer any question of being for or against academic rank. "The big question lies in how to arrange, organize, and balance this distinction in the hundreds of junior colleges all over the country." If the head of a junior college is called president as are heads of senior colleges, then teachers in junior colleges are properly entitled to rank. Included are a list of academic titles and specifications for each.

Hadley, S. Trevor. "The Pros and Cons of Professional Ranking." *Educational Administration and Supervision,* 35:354–362, October, 1949.

Having studied seventy-one replies from colleges with rank and seventy-nine replies from colleges without rank, the author concludes that: (1) faculties without rank are about equally divided in their attitude toward its possible adoption; (2) faculties are reluctant to eliminate ranking where it is now used; (3) those with doctorates favor its adoption; (4) those who favor it do so only because its use is so prevalent; and (5) those not in favor of ranking emphasize the social caste system it often inspires.

Harrington, John C. "Academic Rank in the Community College." *Junior College Journal,* 35:24–27, March, 1965.

A report of a survey of the attitudes and policies held by various officials in state departments and state junior college associations. Replies from respondents ranged from: "Only an aping of four-year institutions" to "Community college teachers have as much right to rank as university teachers teaching in the lower division."

Hendrix, Vernon L. "Academic Rank Revisited." *Junior College Journal,* 35:24–28, February, 1965.

Given the research reported in the article, this author summarizes: ". . . the presence or absence of academic rank policies appears not only to differentiate faculty characteristics but also affects the environment (curricular and extracurricular) as it is perceived by students."

Martin, Clyde V. "The Changing Function of the Public Junior College in California." *Journal of Higher Education,* 29:503–506, December, 1958.

Writing about the weaknesses of the junior college in California, the writer has this to say about rank: ". . . it has been difficult to attract and retain aspiring young instructors of high competence because of the absence of a professorial ranking system. One begins and ends as an instructor. One may advance in terms of salary, but one is prevented from enjoying the prestige and privileges that come with advanced rank. In the academic world, as in the military, rank has its privileges!"

Medsker, Leland L. *The Junior College: Progress and Prospect.* New York: McGraw-Hill Book Company, 1960. Pp. 193–194.

The desire to adopt a system of academic rank is greatest among those teachers who apparently want the junior college to have some of the earmarks of the four-year institution. The author suggests that the question can be raised as to whether a system of rank would tend to further reduce the differences between two-year and four-year colleges.

Punke, Harold H. "Ranking, Tenure, and Sex of Junior-College Faculties." *School Review,* 62:480–487, November, 1954.

A report of the results of a survey of 448 junior colleges. Rank followed the typical university pattern at 21.3 per cent of the institutions. The author presents the factors given in deciding rank, reasons for the use of a ranking system, the length of time that ranking policies had been followed, and changes that respondents anticipated in ranking procedures. Eighty-five per cent of the respondents anticipated no change in ranking policies, while 6 per cent indicated that ranking would change toward placing more emphasis upon "academic status."

Rudolph, Frederick. *The American College and University.* New York: Alfred A. Knopf, 1962. Pp. 398–399.

Colleges established ascending ranks during the 1880's and 1890's because of the "proliferation of knowledge" and increases in enrollment. Ranking was an effort to provide organization needed to deal efficiently with expansion of the institutions. In 1891, Harper at Chicago "began at the bottom with five different grades of one-year appointments. . . . Above these . . . were associates with two-year appointments, instructors with three-year appointments, and assistant professors with four-year appointments; and above them were three grades of permanent appointees: associate professors, professors, and head professors."

Tillery, Dale. "Academic Rank: Promise or Peril?" *Junior College Journal,* 33:6–9, February, 1963.

The question of academic rank for junior college faculties is an attempt by faculty members to define their status in the "hierarchy of education." Rank must be provided only if it aids an institution in achieving its goals. The author believes that a system of ranking contains forces which could undermine the comprehensive features which make the junior college unique.

Wright, Robert L. "A Study of Rank in American Higher Education." *Junior College Journal,* 27:146–149, November, 1956.

The author sampled various college catalogs and bulletins to determine the prevalence of the concepts of academic rank. Rank may give an indication of the importance of prestige in the institutions as well as indicating the measure to which an individual institution patterns itself after the traditions of higher education. The author makes the generalization "that prestige factors involving rank are generally most important in four-year institutions and least important in junior colleges."

VII. Community Junior College Facilities

Barthelme, Donald. "Educational Thoroughfare." *Junior College Journal,* 33:16–20, January, 1963.

A stimulating and interesting paper given at the Rice University Junior-Community College Planning Conference. Among Barthelme's ideas: Properly emphasized, architecture seeks to get out of people's way; "Architecture can teach," in many ways.

Blocker, Clyde E. "The Role of the Administrator in Community College Plant Planning." *Junior College Journal,* 31:326–330, February, 1961.

The central role in developing educational needs into physical facilities is played by the administrator. However, the writer believes that faculty, students, and board have important responsibilities in some aspects of the planning process.

Bursch, Charles, Dow Patterson, and Ruel Taylor. "Plant Facilities for a Community College." *The School Executive,* 69:53–54, December, 1949.

Plant facilities must provide flexibility that will permit change in enrollments, technology, and basic equipment. The space must lend itself to group discussions, operating machines, and individual study. "If maximum service to an entire community is to be realized by a community college plant, designers should not miss any opportunity to facilitate interplay among the college and community groups, business firms, and individuals."

Community College Research Symposium: The Community College Buildings and Facilities. Proceedings of a symposium held in Seattle, Washington, February 8–9, 1963. Olympia, Wash.: State Superintendent of Public Instruction, 1963. Pp. 132–156.

Two research papers, with accompanying discussions, on community college plant and facility planning are presented. Arising out of both papers and discussion is the theme of recognizing the community college as a unique institution. If its job is different from that of the high school and from that of the four-year college, then its facilities and buildings should be designed specifically to fit the functional needs of the community college programs. The admonition is for exhaustive, careful study of program philosophy needs merging with practical space needs to culminate in functional, practical, individualized community college buildings and facilities.

Design for ETV: Planning for Schools with Television. Prepared by Dave Chapman, Inc., Industrial Design for Educational Facilities Laboratories. New York: Educational Facilities Laboratories, 1960. 96 pp.

Methods and designs for educational television facilities are suggested for various shapes and sizes of spaces for maximum use according to function. Some aspects of existing ETV facilities are presented, such as layouts, seating arrangements, and research results.

Giles, Frederic T. "Guidelines for Junior College Campus Planning." *Junior College Journal,* 32:471–475, April, 1962.

A jury of junior college planners suggests guidelines for junior college campus planning. These guidelines recommend that facilities be planned to implement program, provide for regular as well as evening and part-time programs, enhance the philosophy of the college, permit community usage without disruption to regular program, and adapt to future changes in enrollment and program.

Gray, John E. "Are You Planning New Buildings?" *Junior College Journal,* 16:149–154, December, 1945.

Presents a list of suggestions which are useful in the planning of new buildings; for example, "Build classrooms of varying size."

Hardesty, Cecil D. "The Junior College Plant." *American School and University,* 18th ed., 1946. Pp. 84–90.

"In the academic field, the school plant conditions the program; in the vocational field, the school plant controls the program. The educational plans for the school should dictate the building plans." The author then presents a discussion of site selection, selection of the architect, and plans for several different junior colleges.

"How to House a Community College." *School Management,* 5:98–102, April, 1961.

A report of an interview with Dr. N. L. Englehart, Jr., and Professor Edward Romieniec. The replies to the questions raised give insight into the reasons for the differences between community colleges and high schools or four-year colleges. Because of its purposes and unique function, the community college needs facilities designed specifically to house its programs.

Lacy, Bill N., ed. *Ten Designs: Community Colleges.* Houston, Texas: Department of Agriculture, Rice University, 1962. 100 pp.

From June 4 through June 14, 1962, ten outstanding architects and fifty advanced students from nine universities accepted invitations to participate in a Design Fete at Rice University. This volume grew out of that conference. Ten advanced designs for community colleges that are designed specifically for the particular site and specifications given to the particular team are given. The goal was to seek new solutions and new concepts both in architecture and in education.

Mayhew, Lewis B., and others. *A Study on Studying: A Report from the Community College Planning Center on Student Study Facilities.* Community College Planning Center, School

Planning Laboratory. Stanford, Calif.: School of Education, Stanford University, n.d. 55 pp.

From the results of a survey of over 700 students in six California community colleges, students' preferences in study facilities are interpreted. Suggestions based on these interpretations are given for designing and locating student study facilities in community colleges.

Merlo, Frank P., and W. Donald Walling. *Guide for Planning Community College Facilities.* Community College Facilities Project, Division of Field Studies and Research, Graduate School of Education, Rutgers—The State University. New Brunswick, N.J.: The University, 1964. 40 pp.

Summarizes steps to be taken in determining the site, size, location, etc. The need for a master plan for ultimate campus size is stressed. Guides are suggested to be used in planning community college buildings, instructional areas, bookstore, library, and so on. The booklet is accompanied by a checklist that summarizes the items to be considered in planning community college facilities.

Morrison, D. G. "Planning Community Junior College Buildings." *Higher Education,* 14:57–59, December, 1957.

The author presents five logical steps in facility planning: (1) Determine the philosophy of community junior colleges in general, the principles upon which this particular college is being founded, and the purposes for which it will operate; (2) Survey the educational needs of the service area; (3) Develop the space requirements for the programs to be housed—describing the kind, amount, and quality of the space needed in terms of the program or activity planned; (4) Develop preliminary plans; (5) Develop working drawings. Throughout his discussion, the author emphasizes the importance of involving all concerned in the actual process of planning.

Patterson, Dow. "Planning the Junior College Site." *American School Board Journal,* 142:30–31, April, 1961.

The size and type of site have an effect on the instructional program. Limited site size could limit enrollment, instructional program, recreational activities, industral arts, and agricultural education.

Planning and Equipping Business Education Classrooms. Bureau of Business Education, California State Department of Education. Sacramento, Calif.: The Department, 1961. 33 pp.

Outlines specific procedures for calculating space and facility requirements in relation to the philosophy and objectives set by the Department. A section deals specifically with junior college space and facility planning.

Sandell, Roland M. "The Besser Technical School." *American School Board Journal,* 148:25–27, March, 1964.

A presentation of the facilities of the Besser Technical School in Alpena, Michigan.

"Serving a Community With Good Design." *Overview,* 3:48–50, June, 1962.

An illustrated report of the Foothill College campus in California.

Starkey, W. F. "A Theatron for Monticello." *Junior College Journal,* 34:12–13, April, 1964.

Describes a multipurpose building at Monticello College which houses a foyer-art gallery, a theater, swimming pool, gymnasium, and faculty offices.

VIII. Research in the Community Junior College

Brick, Michael. *The Need for Higher Education Facilities in the Mohawk Valley.* A Report to the President and Board of Trustees of the State University of New York. Oneida, N.Y.: The Oneida County Executive and Board of Supervisors, and the Committee on Higher Education of Herkimer, Oneida, and Madison Counties, 1965. 66 pp.

A well-organized, succinct study of the need for additional public higher educational facilities in the Mohawk Valley. The study clearly indicates that need does exist, and recommends that "A state-supported, upper-division institution would best fulfill the educational needs of the Mohawk Valley Area and should be established immediately."

Chomitz, David L. *Business Education for Adults in the Junior College.* Monograph C-5. Cincinnati, Ohio: South-Western Publishing Company, 1957. 56 pp.

An orderly, straightforward study of the status of adult business education in the junior colleges done by the author as his doctoral project at Teachers College, Columbia University. Using the jury method, he developed eighteen conditions conducive to effective business education for adults in the junior colleges. His conclusions and recommendations are sound and valuable to anyone concerned with this phase of higher education.

Community College Research Symposium: Evaluation-Research in the Community College. Proceedings of a Symposium held in Seattle, Washington, February 8–9, 1963. Olympia, Wash.: State Superintendent of Public Instruction, 1963. Pp. 157–165.

The director of research for the State Department of Education summarizes the symposium. In a very clear-cut presentation the different categories of research are delineated and the manner in which community college research fits into these categories is set forth. The community college research program must be unique, just as its role is also unique. In meeting this requirement, standards must be used in evaluating the institution and its program. A series of categories are set up by the author within which such standards need to be set in a realistic manner. The need for long-range planning and inter-institutional cooperation is also stressed.

Dressel, Paul L. *Evaluation in General Education.* Dubuque, Iowa: William C. Brown Company, 1954. 333 pp.

A series of reports of general education evaluation practices in several colleges and universities, including two junior colleges, one public and one private.

Jenkins, Harry E., and Jesse P. Bogue. *A Guide for Self-Evaluation of Junior Colleges.* Washington, D.C.: American Association of Junior Colleges, 1954. 26 pp.

A valuable guide instrument that may be used to assist junior colleges in making self-studies. Each of thirteen schedules is presented with various individual items and provisions for ratings on it. A scale of values based on percentages makes it possible to draw a profile line for each schedule.

Johnson, B. Lamar. *Islands of Innovation.* Occasional Report Number 6, UCLA Junior College Leadership Program. Los Angeles: University of California, Los Angeles, 1964. 80 pp.

Reports on an exploration into the methods and devices used by community junior colleges in seeking to increase the effectiveness of their faculty services. Among the innovations and experiments indicated by the junior colleges surveyed were teaching aides, consultants, programed instruction, both open- and closed-circuit TV, executive telephone hook-ups, video tape recorders, instructional resource centers, year-round calendars, inter-institutional pooling of faculty and facilities, and many others.

Johnson, B. Lamar, ed. *New Directions for Instruction in the Junior College.* Occasional Report Number 7, UCLA Junior College Leadership Program. Los Angeles: University of California, Los Angeles, 1964. 132 pp.

Reporting on the eighth in a series of summer conferences sponsored jointly by the University of California, Los Angeles, the Accrediting Commission for Junior Colleges of the Western Association of Schools and Colleges, and the American Association of Junior Colleges, Johnson expresses the hope that the report will "stimulate innovation and experimentation in instruction."

Addresses by some of the top leaders in community junior college education deal with changes in such areas as the preparation of junior college instructors, instruction in nursing, innovations suggested by experimental colleges, the utilization of programed instruction, educational television, and inter-institutional cooperation.

Knoell, Dorothy M., and Leland L. Medsker. *From Junior to Senior College: A National Study of the Transfer Student.* Washington, D.C.: American Council on Education, 1965. 102 pp.

As the college potential group grows in size, the junior college will increasingly become the stepping stone to the four-year college through a transfer program. What happens to transfer students? How well do they do academically? What factors determine their success? These and many other questions are studied in this report. The study involved over 10,000 students in 345 two-year colleges and 43 senior colleges and universities. It has implications for administrators, guidance counsellors, admissions officers, and parents.

Marsee, Stuart E. "A President's View of Institutional Research." *Junior College Journal,* 35:24–25, May, 1965.

While the community junior college is constantly referred to as a teaching institution as opposed to research, the author here indicates that institutional research is absolutely essential to provide the bases upon which sound decisions can be made. Junior college instructors, freed from the "publish or perish" dictum, are able to participate in an institutional research program with a feeling of keen interest rather than of compulsion. The author indicates some of the areas that require continuous attention through research activities in order that the institution may operate efficiently and grow in stature.

Morrison, Donald G. "Research and the Two-Year College." *Junior College Journal,* 29:128–132, November, 1958.

The types of research done in two-year colleges are reviewed in this article. The future role of the two-year college in what is essentially institutional research is indicated.

O'Connor, Thomas J. *Follow-up Studies in Junior Colleges: A Tool for Institutional Improvement.* Washington, D.C.: American Association of Junior Colleges, 1965. 75 pp.

Gives clear, step-by-step procedures for conducting follow-up studies. Provides successful examples of survey and questionnaire instruments. Stresses the vital role such information plays in the strengthening, developing, and revising of the community junior college curriculum. It is only through such follow-up procedures that the college can determine its effectiveness in meeting the needs of its students.

"Recent Research." *Junior College Journal,* 34:38–39, March, 1964.

Presents a selected list of dissertations recently completed or under way that are specifically related to the community junior college, as reported by ten university centers participating in the Junior College Leadership Program.

Richards, James M., Jr., Lorraine M. Rand, and Leonard P. Rand. *A Description of Junior Colleges.* ACT Research Report No. 5. Iowa City, Iowa: Research and Development Division, American College Testing Program, July, 1965. 27 pp.

Report of a study whose primary goal was to build up a profile to be "used to characterize junior colleges, and which will make possible more efficient research into the effects of junior colleges on their students." From an original list of thirty-six characteristics, just six "rotated factors" evolved: (1) cultural affluence, (2) technological specialization, (3) size, (4) age, (5) transfer emphasis, and (6) business orientation.

The authors note the absence of such studies despite the rapid expansion of two-year colleges. They indicate the great need for some type of profile that will show the ways in which different colleges affect student accomplishment and growth.

Richards, James M., Jr., Leonard P. Rand, and Lorraine M. Rand. *Regional Differences in Junior Colleges.* ACT Research Report No. 9. Iowa City, Iowa: Research and Development Division, American College Testing Program, December, 1965. 17 pp.

Examines the geographical distribution of six categories of junior college characteristics derived from a previous computation from 581 accredited junior colleges. The results of the study, it is hoped, will prove valuable in providing sound alternatives for the orderly development of junior colleges in light of their characteristics and geographic location. Should be of great value to counsellors, administrators, and board members.

Schenz, R. F. "What is Done for the Low Ability Students? Report on a Recent National Study of Junior College Courses and Curriculums." *Junior College Journal,* 34:22–27, May, 1964.

On the basis of his investigations, the author concludes that (1) the remedial function is accepted by the administrators of junior colleges as a legitimate function for these institutions; (2) administrators of junior colleges accept the responsibility of providing courses and curriculums to meet the needs of students with low ability; (3) emerging throughout the nation is an awareness on the part of junior college administrators of the problem of meeting the needs of students with low ability.

"A Study of Income and Expenditure Patterns Among Twenty-Four (24) Independent and Church-Related Junior Colleges: Year 1962–3." Wellesley, Mass.: Pine Manor Junior College, 1965. 152 pp.

Conducted under a grant from the U.S. Office of Education under the Cooperative Research Program, this study was designed to provide comparative financial information to private junior colleges. Data were collected from twenty-four independent and church-related colleges and broken down into four general categories, and guides were constructed from the analyses. A pioneering effort to fill a real need.

Wattenbarger, James L., and Winfred L. Godwin, eds. *The Community College in the South: Progress and Prospects.* Committee on Education Beyond the High School, Southern States Work Conference. Tallahassee, Fla.: State Education Department, 1962. 132 pp.

The committee's objective, as reported by Wattenbarger, was to suggest patterns of operation and methods of study which each of the southern states might consider in its efforts to provide a variety of post-secondary, but less than baccalaureate, education for increasing numbers of its youth. Among the topics that were dealt with by the committee were: impending developments relating to two-year colleges in the various states; state-wide planning; legal status of junior colleges; current research on community junior colleges; current research on community junior college students; and the preparation of faculty for the junior colleges.

Index of Authors